Bird Watching - on beach and mud flats

Turnstone

Always busy on the strand line of pebbly beaches such as Longrock looking for sand hoppers and other delicacies. Curious skeletal markings on their back and wings make them look like flying ghosts.

Heron

Nests at Marazion marsh and sometimes seen fishing on Longrock beach in the evenings.

Oystercatcher

Usually seen feeding on sandy beaches but can be found at high tide grubbing up worms at traffic roundabouts. Magnificent orange beak and lovely call - a long 'peeep'. Known locally as the sea-pie.

Curlew

Curlew (whimbrel similar) Large flocks can be seen at most times of year on the muddy estuaries. A very distinctive drawn out call of 'coor-lee'.

Little Egret

A member of the heron family and an increasingly common sight in Hayle estuary.

Places to visit

Land's End

Spring and autumn are probably the best times to see migrant birds here. There are regular rarities - some blown across the Atlantic by storms. Also RSPB Discovery Centre.

Armed Knight

Island just south of Land's End - breeding place for guillemots and razorbills. Good vantage point from the cliff at Carn Greeb but you will need good binoculars. Best in spring to early summer.

The Island, St Ives

Good for passage migrants in spring and autumn and when northerly winds bring birds in-shore - gannets are sometimes seen diving at Porthminster.

Marazion Marsh

Home to many thousands of Baltic starlings in the winter. Guided walks in the summer - ring Pz TIC for details telephone (01736) 362207 or visit - www.rspb.org.uk/reserves and navigate to Marazion Marsh

Hayle Estuary

The estuary is well known for its bird life - especially waders such as Little Egrets. The best time to watch is at high water as the incoming sea pushes the birds out of the estuary channels -www.rspb.org.uk/reserves

and navigate to Hayle estuary

Paradise Park, Hayle

Wildlife park and tropical bird gardens with adventure playgrounds and indoor play centre - info T: (01736) 751020 www.paradisepark.org.uk

Wildlife safari

Fast boat safari in search of dolphins, seals and basking sharks - they also do overland tours on the moors.
T: (01736) 811 200
www.elementaltours.co.uk

More Info

The best book on local wildlife is *A Natural History of Land's End* by Jean Lawman

Getting your bearings

The Armed Knight near Land's End

One of the best ways to start exploring the area is to get your bearings from one of the higher hills such as Trencrom, Sancreed Beacon, Chapel Carn Brea or Carn Galva. Broadly speaking, the peninsula is shaped like a giant wedge, with a crescent of exposed hills and moorland on the north and west coasts. To the south and east lies the sheltered farmland and safe anchorage of Mount's Bay. The bias of high ground to the north means the northward flowing streams sometimes have only to travel a few hundred metres before they tumble into the sea. The southerly streams, by contrast, flow for four or five miles into the green wooded valleys of Lamorna, St Loy and Penberth. You might also consider a drive along the coast road from St Just to St Ives which takes in many of the most impressive parts of the peninsula or even better, take the number 300 open-top bus, which gives spectacular views.

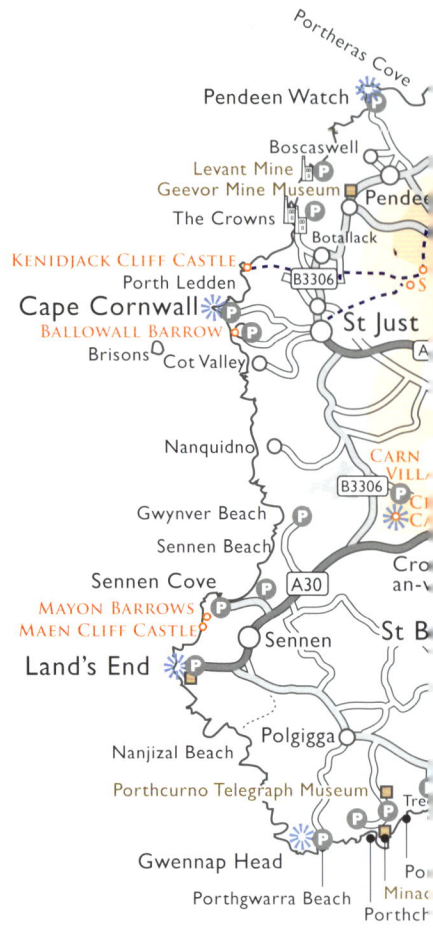

Basic Information

Tourist Information

St Ives TIC, The Guildhall.
T: (01736) 796297
E: ivtic@penwith.gov.
Penzance TIC, The bus/train
station T: (01736) 362207
E: pztic@penwith.gov.uk
There are also smaller offices at
Hayle & St Just.

Boats trips

Boat trips leave from Penzance
harbour to view St Michael's
Mount & Lamorna and to
watch seals. Boats also leave
from St Ives harbour to view
the north coast and to seal
watch.

Top Tips

Never try to park in St Ives
during the season - always take
the train which has spectacular
views. Watch out for seagulls
in St Ives who will snatch food
from your hand. Avoid tourist
attractions on overcast days if
you don't like crowds.

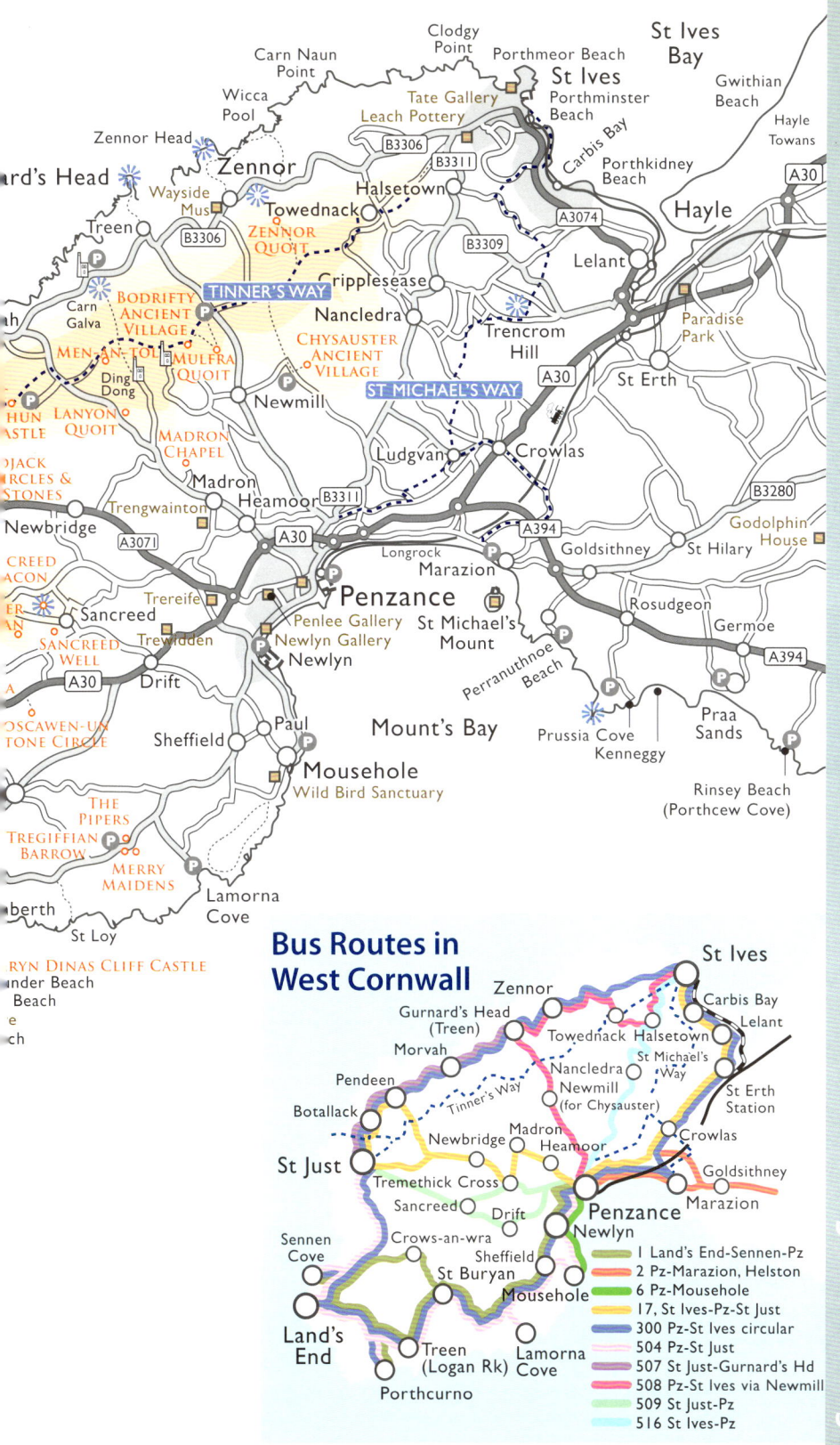

Bus Routes in West Cornwall

1 Land's End-Sennen-Pz
2 Pz-Marazion, Helston
6 Pz-Mousehole
17, St Ives-Pz-St Just
300 Pz-St Ives circular
504 Pz-St Just
507 St Just-Gurnard's Hd
508 Pz-St Ives via Newmill
509 St Just-Pz
516 St Ives-Pz

West Cornwall Beaches

Beach Mad with Kids

Children will be happy on almost any beach in West Cornwall but small children may find it difficult to negotiate the steep climbs to the more isolated beaches such as Pedn and Rinsey. They can also find the powerful waves at Porthcurno and Sennen off-putting - so try the more sheltered beaches such as Perranuthnoe and Marazion. We've shown the beaches that have lifeguards during the tourist season and, probably more important, the beaches where you can buy ice-creams. Many of the most popular beaches, such as Sennen and the St Ives beaches, can become unpleasantly busy during the school holidays but you don't have to walk far to find somewhere more deserted. Most harbours such as St Ives and Mousehole will have a small patch of sand with the added bonus of shops, parking and ice cream close to hand. Older children (& parents) can get surfing lessons at Sennen and St Ives.

If you go to just one beach....

Go to Pedn Vounder

Surf Mad

By far the most consistent surf can be found at Sennen, Gwynver and at Porthmeor beach in St Ives. There are surf schools at Sennen and St Ives. Sennen and Gwynver are the most exposed beaches - the waves here can be surprisingly strong for the unwary.

Surf Info

www.cornwalls.co.uk/surfing

Loose the Crowds

You don't have to walk that far to find a deserted beach even in the school holidays. Best would be Nanjizal which is 10-15 minutes walk from Trevilley and Kenneggy near Praa Sands - both difficult to reach. Portheras and Porthmeor (Pendeen) are the best on the north coast. Needless to say, none have facilities.

Guide to symbols

🏳	Lifeguards in the summer	🏄	Good for surf dudes
Ⓟ	Parking	🏕	Campsite close by
♿	Level access	🛏	B&B/Hotels close by
👪	Good for families	🚻	Toilets nearby
🚌 2	On bus route	🐕	All-year dog beach (otherwise
🛍	Shopping		dog ban between 8am & 7pm
☕	Cup of tea nearby		1st May to end September
🍽	Proper sit down meals nearby		

Beach Guide - clockwise from Mount's Bay to St Ives Bay

Longrock beach

Rinsey Cove (Porthcew)
Ⓟ 👪

Sublime, little known beach. Slightly awkward climb over rocks down onto beach. Sand only at low water although people swim off the rocks at high water. 10 minute walk down cliff from National Trust car park at Rinsey. Take turning off A394 (Penzance to Helston road) at Ashton. No facilities.

Praa Sands
🏳️ Ⓟ ♿ 👪 🚌 2 🚕 ▼🍴
🏄 ⛺ 🐕 👫

Large, busy family beach with soft sand. All facilities close at hand.

Prussia Cove
Ⓟ (limited so get there early) 👪 🐕

Actually two small secluded pebbly coves - Bessy's Cove & King's Cove. The walk from the cliff top car park often puts people off, so these beaches are not usually too busy, although the small car park fills up quickly. No beach at high water & no facilities. Take turning off A394 (Penzance to Helston road) at Rosudgeon.

Kenneggy Sands
Ⓟ (Prussia Cove) 👪 🐕

Path from cliff top now officially closed because of difficult descent to beach by rope. Access by crossing the rocks at low water - beware of incoming tide. No facilities.

Perranuthnoe
Ⓟ ♿ 👪 🚌 2 ▼🚕🐕

Favourite of many local families. Tends to be less crowded than the more spectacular beaches of Porthcurno and Sennen. Small cafe & good parking. No sand at high water.

Marazion & Longrock
🏳️ Ⓟ ♿ 👪 🚌 (numerous buses) 🚕▼ 🍴⛺🐕 (Longrock) 👫

Wide beaches - never really busy - good for families with small children. Marazion has a good children's playground next to the beach and during the summer there are fair rides set up on the Green. Can sit in the Godolphin pub and watch children on beach. All facilities. Longrock is quieter - car park on seaward side of train tracks - turn opposite the entrance to Longrock Industrial Estate.

Mousehole
Ⓟ 👪 🚌 6,504 🚕▼ 🍴🐕 👫

There is a small sea-filled pool and pebbly beach on the Newlyn side of the Old Coastguard Hotel. The harbour has enough sand for little children to play.

Pedn Vounder
Ⓟ 🚌 1,300 ▼& 🍴 at Treen) ⛺

One of the best beaches in Britain. Park at Treen. It's a 10 minute walk down the lane past the camp site to Treen Cliff. Cross straight over the main coast path and follow the winding path down to the beach. Descent from Treen Cliff to the beach is steep and the last part involves some rock climbing. However, the rocky descent appears more difficult than it really is. It's a good idea to carry everything in a back pack so that your hands are kept free. This is probably not a good choice for parents with very small children or for people unsteady on their legs. Pedn is an unofficial naturist beach. Not much beach at high water. No facilities. Very highly recommended.

Porthcurno
🏳️ Ⓟ ♿ 👪 🚌 1,300,504 🚕▼🍴 🏄🚕 ⛺🐕 👫

Photo on front cover. Perfect family beach. Extremely popular beach with fine, soft, shell sand even at high water. The beach shelves away steeply and is quite exposed so

Pedn Vounder beach with Treryn Dinas in the background

swimming can be difficult in a rough sea. Children love to play in the small stream at the top of the beach. There is a large car park above the beach but get here early on sunny days to ensure a parking space. Adjacent to the Minack Theatre and the Museum of Telegraphy. All facilities. Highly recommended for families.

Porthchapel

Small steeply shelving beach below St Levan Church. Drive through Porthcurno, past the Minack Theatre and just as the church comes into view parking is up a small lane on the right in a field. Footpath to the beach is just opposite car park turning - it's about 600m to the beach. The path down to the beach is a bit of a scramble.

No facilities. Usually some sand even at high water.

Porthgwarra

Sweet, tiny sheltered beach in the lee of Gwennap Head. Looses the sun in late afternoon. Good access to Gwennap Head for walks and wildlife. No beach at high water. Car Park, toilets and small cafe shop.

Nanjizal

A popular beach in the 1960's before the sand was swept away in a series of bad storms. There are signs that the sand is coming back. Wonderfully deserted with large beach exposed at low water. Popular to swim in the deep pool under the natural rock arch on the

east side of the beach. It's a 20 minute walk across the fields from the lay-by near Trevescan on the B3315 or alternatively, walk around from Land's End. Wreck shows at low spring tide under Carn Boel. Little beach at high water. No facilities. Highly recommended for isolated back-to-nature freaks.

Cape Cornwall - Priest's Cove

Small tidal pool on the south side of the Cape and some sand at low water.

Sennen Cove

Large expanse of golden sand and the favourite beach of many in West Cornwall. It's exposed and gets powerful waves so it's excellent for body boards & surfing. Car park fills up quickly but overflow parking is available on the top of the cliff at Mayon Green (a steep walk down to the beach). Little beach at high water. Many people take barbecues for the evening when the beach quickly empties. All facilities. Highly recommended family beach.

Porthchapel

Nanjizal beach

Gwynver Beach

Top beach for surfers. Steep walk down from the small car park on top of the cliff. Take the turning near Escalls Methodist Chapel where a sign advertises Tregiffian Farm self catering units. No Facilities. Highly recommended for surf bums.

Portheras Cove

(P) (Pubs in Pendeen) (Manor Farm)

Photo on page 44. Deserted, sandy beach at low water. Beware razor sharp fragments of old wreck under the sand - its suggested that you wear beach shoes at all times - even when swimming. There are always seals to be seen here. Park at Pendeen Lighthouse & walk along coast or park at Chypraze Farm on the cliff above the beach. No facilities except for teas at Manor Farm above Pendeen Lighthouse.

Porthmeor (Pendeen)

300 (Gurnard's Head Pub)

Deserted, sandy beach.

St Ives - Porthmeor

(P)(Balnoon) (Ayr Pk)

Glorious sandy beach below the Tate Gallery. Great surfing. Gets very busy in the summer. Parking is impossible in St Ives in July & August so all St Ives beaches are best avoided unless you are staying within walking distance. If you do want to come to St Ives, it's easier to visit by train. All facilities. Highly recommended for art loving surf bums & families.

St Ives - Porthgwidden

Small, sheltered beach tucked around the corner from Porthmeor (see above). All facilities.

St Ives - the Harbour

Large sheltered, sandy beach. All facilities.

St Ives - Porthminster

(P) (Station)

Large sheltered, sandy beach below train station. Great cafe above beach. All facilities.

Carbis Bay

(P) 17

See below - all facilities.

Carbis Bay

Porth Kidney Sands

(P)(Lelant Church on road)

Huge sandy beach backed by sheltered dunes. Always empty. Limited parking at Lelant Church. 10 minute walk over golf course and dunes. Dangerous to swim in the river. No facilities.

Sennen beach

A kingdom of granite cliffs & moors

Looking east from Carn Galva over the pattern of ancient fields

A granite kingdom

The granite of the Land's End peninsula has two vital qualities that have shaped the lives of the people that have lived here; it provides a durable stone for quarrying and building - so durable that some prehistoric houses and field boundaries are still clearly visible after 6,000 years - and it contains the mineral veins, or lodes, of tin and copper that have been mined continuously for the last 3,000 years.

The Land's End peninsula is essentially a large dome-shaped bulb of granite set in an older surrounding sea of slates - part of a chain of similar intrusions that run broadly east to west from Dartmoor to the Isles of Scilly.

The granite was implanted as a molten mass into the base of a now lost mountain range about 300 million years ago as a consequence of a collision of continental plates. Over millions of years the overlying slates have been worn away exposing the granite at the surface. The slates now only form a fringe around the coast of the peninsula. This is very obvious on the north coast where they form a narrow, flat shelf a few fields wide below Carn Galva & Zennor Hill.

A strong characteristic of soils that overlie granite bedrock are the large boulders or moorstones that sit on the surface even in cultivated fields. It is assumed that many of the stone field walls date from the Neolithic period (4000-2500BC) when agriculture was first practised here.

Another characteristic of the granite bedrock are the huge cubic blocks precariously stacked one on another, that form the rocky crags or carns. The cubic system of joints was formed deep underground as the molten granite slowly cooled, shrunk and fractured. Once the granite is exposed, the natural weathering process erodes the rock along these lines of weakness until huge blocks weighing many tons may rest on a tiny point of contact with the block below. These stones can then sometimes be rocked backwards and forwards and are called *logan* or rocking stones. The most famous is the Logan Rock near Treen on the south coast, (section 3). A smaller example is the logan stone at Bosigran just inside Bosigran Iron Age cliff castle (section 6).

The carns can often take on strange anthropomorphic shapes and many are named after animals such as The Horseback near Zennor and the Gurnard's Head near Treen on the north coast. Locals stories tell how the rocks come alive in the frequent swirling sea mists that drift in from the Atlantic.

Gwennap Head

An ancient realm

In a peninsula that is already rich in prehistoric remains, the north coast from Zennor to St Just is exceptional - to the extent that it is still a predominantly prehistoric landscape - a tapestry of prehistoric settlements, field boundaries, fortifications and sacred sites. In many places the original Bronze and Iron Age houses and villages are preserved such as Bodrifty and Chysauster. What makes it particularly special is that so much of the accompanying prehistoric landscape has survived too. Nowhere in Britain are you more acutely aware of the presence of prehistoric man, almost as if you turned suddenly you might catch a glimpse of one of them out of the corner of your eye.

A Celtic Land

There is something not altogether benign about the cliffs and treeless moors of West Cornwall. It can sometimes feel intimidating - everywhere the granite bedrock restlessly breaks through the surface, frustrating attempts at taming and cultivating the land.

Here on the Penwith moors you can sit beneath any number of Stone Age burial tombs such as Mulfra Quoit, Lanyon Quoit and Chun Quoit; at Bodrifty you can walk amongst the round houses and field walls of the Bronze Age

people who farmed this landscape 3,500 years ago; at the Merry Maidens and Boscawen-un sit within their ritual stone circles; at Chysauster and Carn Euny you can wander around the courtyard houses of the Iron Age Celts; at Trencrom and Logan Rock sit within their defensive forts; at Madron Well and Sancreed Well sit in the tiny chapels of the Cornish saints who brought Christianity to the Cornish 1,400 years ago.

The tough landscape seems to foster a continuity between past and present. The Celts believed the numerous tiny springs were passageways to an underworld. Later as Christianity took root they became holy wells and inherited this earlier pagan symbolism. This continuous thread of belief has lasted to the present day - Sancreed Well and Madron Well are still 'dressed' by locals.

Industry has also become meshed with mythology. The gaping mine shafts that pepper the landscape mimic the holy wells as dark entrances to a Celtic underworld. Miles of tunnels and galleries meander beneath the moors supposedly inhabited by the mischievous little people or *spiggins* of Celtic legend. Drainage tunnels or adits from long abandoned mines driven into the side of cliffs still disgorge rust soaked fluids onto the beaches.

Guide to the Ancient Sites
The Stone Age - 4000 to 2500BC

Chun Quoit overlooking the north coast

Monument builders & farmers

About 6,000 years ago new ideas and a new group of people slowly moved into West Cornwall - these were the Neolithic peoples. They were farmers rather than nomads and probably crossed into Britain from Europe sometime after the end of the last Ice Age, 10,000 years ago. The Ice Age had made Britain inhospitable, but as the climate moderated, so sub-arctic tundra gave way to the more temperate forest and grasslands we are familiar with today. This more settled way of life seems to have allowed rank and status to become more important and for the first time tombs and monuments are constructed in the landscape.

Field boundaries

These are the first man-made structures in West Cornwall - created as the land was systematically cleared of stones. Most date from before the pyramids.

Fortified sites

There is no conclusive evidence of Neolithic forts in West Cornwall although it is thought that Trencrom Hill and Carn Galva are both Neolithic sites. They certainly follow a pattern of seeking out dramatic rocky situations seen in other proven Neolithic sites.

Quoits - chamber tombs

The Penwith chamber tombs known locally as *quoits* were constructed about 5,000 years ago. A number of fine examples of these burial tombs stand on the chain of the hills above the north coast - on the route of Tinner's Way (see p46).

Barrows - entrance graves

A second, later wave of settlers built the Scillonian chamber tombs or entrance graves that are particular to West Cornwall and the Isles of Scilly. The best example being Tregiffian Barrow near to the Merry Maidens stone circle.

Stone Age Sites in West Cornwall

Ancient field walls at Land's End

Field Boundaries, Land's End (4)

The Stone Age peoples were the first to clear the land and start to cultivate. In West Cornwall that means clearing the large boulders that naturally litter the surface. For this reason the oldest walls are thought to be those with the biggest boulders in them. The field walls pictured above are near to Land's End but could equally be any along the north coast. Park either at Land's End (entrance fee) or at Sennen.

Ballowall Barrow, Carn Gluz, St just (6)

Ballowall Barrow near St Just

Lost for a number of years under the spoil heaps of a tin mine. A unique barrow with a complex history and a number of burial cists (stone lined boxes). Take the Cape Cornwall road from St Just, past the school and then turn left at the sign to Carn Gloose. Parking is on the cliff top. You can walk north to Cape Cornwall or south to Cot Valley and its tin mining ruins.

Tregiffian Barrow (2)

Scillonian Entrance Grave so close to the road that it has to make a diversion round. Part of a concentration of monuments around the later Bronze Age monuments of the Merry Maidens stone circle and the Pipers standing stones. Note the stone with numerous cup-like depressions cut in the top. This mimics a natural weathering phenomenon found on the most exposed granite outcrops (Carn Galva) where the cups have all sorts of druidic legends attributed to them.

Lanyon Quoit (7)

Most famous of the Land's End chamber tombs or quoits. Midway between Madron & Morvah. Picture page 49.

Mulfra Quoit (7)*

Magnificently sited quoit overlooking Mount's Bay. Numerous footpaths to other local sites such as Bodrifty Prehistoric Village.

Tregiffian Barrow near Lamorna

Chun Quoit (7)*

The first and best preserved in a string of Stone Age chamber tombs on the sides of hills above the north coast. This one is almost undamaged - only missing the covering mound of earth & stones. Below the later Iron Age hill fort of Chun Castle. Parking just off the B3318 as it forks to Pendeen and Trewellard. Also within reach of Kenidjack Carn.

Mulfra Quoit with its view over Mount's Bay

This list only represents the best and most accessible sites. (6) refers to the relevant section in this book & sites shown * are on the route of the Tinner's Way.

Guide to the Ancient Sites
The Bronze Age - 2500 to 600BC

Boscawen-un Circle - the most intriguing and atmospheric of West Cornwall stone circles

Star Gazers & Stone Circles

The people of the Bronze Age brought a knowledge of metal working to West Cornwall. They started to mine the copper veins in the cliffs and the tin deposits in the stream beds to make tools, jewellery and weapons.

It was at this time the stone circles and standing stones (menhirs) were constructed. Their monuments obviously had some important religious or ritualistic symbolism considering the immense effort needed to assemble and erect them.

The Bronze age peoples appear to have studied the stars closely. The circles at Merry Maidens (Lamorna) and Boscawen-un both have 19 stones - this may correspond to the procession of the moon's orbit over a roughly 19-year period or could be the 19-year cycle where the solar and lunar cycles converge. Whatever the truth, the best

and most atmospheric stone circle is at Boscawen-un, just outside Penzance off the A30 between Drift and Crows-an-wra. The best time to visit is very early in the morning or at sun set.

Burial mounds and cists

The Bronze Age people also constructed burial mounds similar to the Scillonian chamber tombs of the Neolithic period, a good example being Mayon Barrow between Sennen and Land's End.

Round Houses

The remains of Bronze Age settlements consisting of hut circles or round houses are very common throughout the area. The best example is Bodrifty Ancient Village near Mulfra Quoit. A reconstructed hut has been built in a nearby field.

Menhirs & Holed stones

Best examples are the Men-an-tol and the Pipers next to the Merry Maidens stone circle.

Bronze Age Sites in West Cornwall

The reconstructed round house at Bodrifty

Men-an-tol (7)*

Holed stone and part of a larger alignment of stones. The opening is large enough for a child to crawl through. Folklore attributes healing properties to the stone. It was said to be able to cure children of rickets. The children had to crawl through the stone nine times towards the setting sun.

Men-an-tol

Boscawen-un Circle

Atmospheric stone circle with axe-like inclined central stone. This stone aligns with the midsummer solstice sunrise and the angled sunlight illuminates two shallow carved axe heads on the base of the stone barely visible normally. Set in a natural dip in the landscape with 19 stones arranged in an oval. One of the stones in the circle is a milk-white quartz that sparkles.

Quartz occurs naturally as pure veins in Cornish rocks (it also gives granite its sparkle) and may mark the entrance as at the Merry Maidens. Used by the Cornish Gorsedd at its first gorseth in 1928. Park at the small roadside layby on A30 - look for the wooden kissing gate in the hedge 0.8km west of Boscawen-noon Farm.

Merry Maidens (2)

The most accessible and well known of West Cornwall circles. 19 equally spaced stones, with a wider, possible entrance, spacing on the north east. The maidens were found dancing on a sabbath and turned to stone for their blasphemy as were the nearby 'pipers'. The large menhirs or pipers are also Bronze Age and the circle looks as if it was part of a larger collection and alignments of

One of the Pipers of Boleigh

monuments including the Stone Age entrance grave of Tregiffian Barrow.

Pipers of Boleigh (2)

Two very large and impressive standing stones - the largest in Cornwall.

Bodrifty Village (7)*

Excavated settlement of hut circles or round houses with a surrounding, low defensive earthwork. Some of the hut circles may date from the late Bronze Age and it was certainly in occupation during the Iron Age. The site makes an interesting contrast with the settlements at Carn Euny

Round house at Bodrifty

and Chysauster whose more sophisticated courtyard houses never seem to have gained the widespread use of the simple round house plan. Invite yourself into one of the houses and take lunch with locals as they did 2,000 years ago. Information display boards around the site. At the time of writing the private reconstructed round house at Bodrifty was open to the public. It is sign posted from the village. Park opposite the Zennor turning on the Penzance/Newmill-Gurnard's Head road near Mulfra Quoit or near the mine at Bodrifty.

This list only represents the best and most accessible sites. (6) refers to the relevant section in this book & sites shown * are on the route of the Tinner's Way.

Guide to the Ancient Sites
The Iron & Romano British Age - 600BC to 600AD

Remains of stores or livestock pens in a courtyard house at Chysauster

Courtyards and Castles

The landscape of the northern coast between Pendeen and St Ives represents a remarkably well preserved Iron Age landscape. Iron Age Celts moved into West Cornwall about 2,500 years ago. They developed a new house form that incorporated the round house of the Bronze Age but developed it further by incorporating storage spaces and workshops into the walls of a secure courtyard. The courtyard house settlements at Chysauster and Carn Euny are of national importance. One of the things that makes them so interesting is the way we can glimpse something of the ordinary lives of our ancestors. The villages are complete to shoulder height only lacking their roofs.

Fogous

A peculiar structure associated with Iron Age villages are the underground passages or fogous. We have no clear idea as to their significance - they may have a religious function or only have been used as a cold stores for food. The best example is at Carn Euny Ancient Village and there is a smaller example at Pendeen.

Forts & cliff castles

The Iron Age was a time of war and strife and almost every good defensive hilltop and headland was fortified. Nearly all the headlands had ramparts constructed across their necks - best examples Treryn Dinas and Mayon castle.

Iron Age Courtyard House

Iron Age Sites in West Cornwall

The ramparts of Mayon cliff castle between Land's End & Sennen

Bosullow Trehyllys (7)

Overgrown courtyard house settlement adjacent to the Tinner's Way and in the protective shadow of Chun Castle. On private land. The farmer will be happy to show you around. The telephone contact number is on a wooden gate at the site. There is a small entrance fee that goes to charity.

Carn Euny Fogou

Trencrom Hillfort (9)

Quite a steep climb to the summit from the National Trust car park but there are great views up the coast to North Cornwall and south to St Michael's Mount. Original entrance to fort marked by upright stone jambs on east side. Defensive walls clearly visible on south & west sides. May have been in use as early as the Stone Age.

Carn Euny

Porthmeor Village (7)

Village of courtyard houses ask at Porthmeor Farm for permission to visit.

Chysauster Ancient Village (8)

Classic, excavated Iron Age village of national importance. Consists of nine courtyard houses and ruined fogou. There are many details of life 2,000 years ago with intact

drains and thresholds. There is often a reenactment of Celtic life in the summer. Entrance fee and guidebook available (includes description of Carn Euny too). Follow signs from B3311 road - back road from St Ives to Penzance.

Carn Euny Ancient Village & Fogou

Small excavated Bronze and Iron Age settlement with fabulous fogou (underground passage). Consists of a number of courtyard and round houses. Children love to run in and out of the houses. Makes an excellent base to explore numerous local antiquities such as Caer Bran hillfort. Also tiny chapel and well of St Euny nearby. Follow the signs from Drift on the A30 west of Penzance. See next page.

Chun Castle (7)*

The best hillfort in West Cornwall. Stands above the late Stone Age Chun Quoit and the Iron Age courtyard settlement at Bosullow Trehyllys. Parking just off the B3318 as it forks to Pendeen and Trewellard.

Mayon Cliff Castle (4)

Iron Age cliff castle.

Treryn Dinas (3)

Iron Age cliff castle.

Chun Castle near Morvah with views south and north

This list only represents the best and most accessible sites. (6) refers to the relevant section in this book & sites shown * are on the route of the Tinner's Way.

Carn Euny Prehistoric Village

Entrance to Courtyard House 2

The majority of the visible remains at Carn Euny date from the Iron Age but unlike the classic courtyard settlement at Chysauster it seems to have evolved in a more organic way. The village incorporates both simple round houses and a variant type of courtyard house which surprisingly lacks the large round house element altogether - but retains the courtyard and small rooms.

What makes Carn Euny very special is the rare underground corbelled chamber and the exceptionally well preserved underground passage or *fogou*. The corbelled chamber and its entrance passage seem to have been the earliest structures - they date from about 500BC. The fogou was built later, cutting the entrance passage at right angles and with its only entrance being via the creep passage at the west end.

The final stage was the opening up of the east end of the passage and the building of the courtyard houses. There has been some speculation that the courtyard houses had some ceremonial function because they do not incorpo-

rate the usual round house in their plan. The paved entrance to Courtyard House 1 is well preserved and feels quite grand and again it is suggested that this was an important ceremonial entrance to the

fogou. Unfortunately, we have very little idea what function a fogou performed.

More info in the English Heritage booklet on sale at Chysauster.

Plan of Carn Euny Village

(map labels) Probably contemporary Prehistoric field walls · Unexcavated area · Paved entrance · Underground corbelled chamber · Creep passage · Courtyard House 1 · Stone workroom · Footpath to St Euny's Holy Well & Bartinney Castle · Stile · Fogou · Culvert for drain · Courtyard House · C'bd · 18th Century Cottage · Courtyard House 2 · Paved entrance & jamb stones · Store/workroom · Paved entrance · Unexcavated area · Round House · Round House · Field boundaries · Kissing gate · Modern entrance from car park · 0 10 20 30ft · 0 10m · Mr D Christie

Plan of Carn Euny Fogou

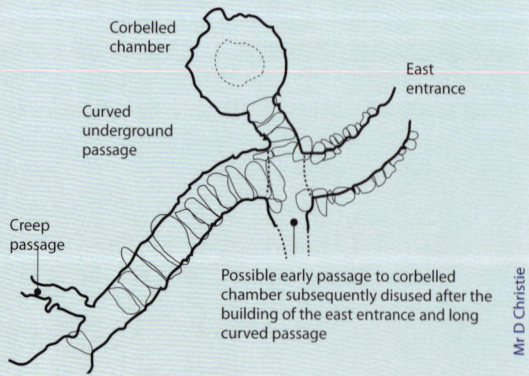

(diagram labels) Corbelled chamber · East entrance · Curved underground passage · Creep passage · Possible early passage to corbelled chamber subsequently disused after the building of the east entrance and long curved passage · Mr D Christie

Guide to the Ancient Sites
The Age of the Cornish Saints - 600AD to 1000AD

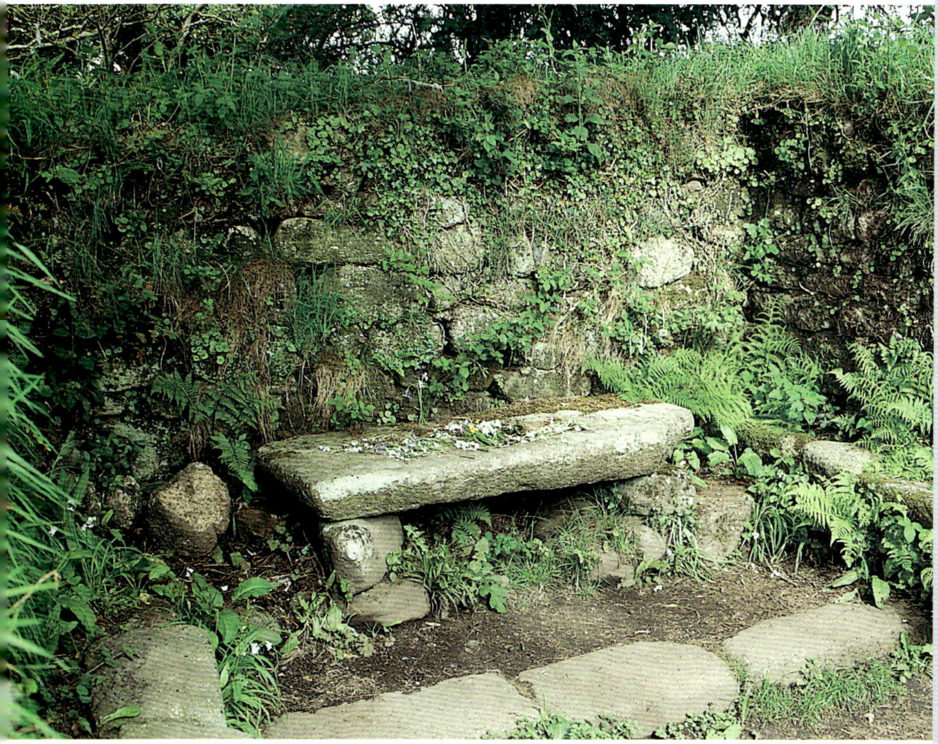

Madron Well - the altar stone - the well is still used for baptisms

Holy Wells & Chapels

From the C6th onwards a wave of Celtic Christian missionaries arrived in Cornwall from Wales and Ireland. The Romans had brought Christianity to Britain but in many places it had died away as Roman influence faded after they left Britain in AD410. What survived in Wales and Ireland was a monastic and hermitic religion. These men and women became the Cornish saints and they found a ready acceptance in these wild western lands. The early saints arrived by sea and set up sacred enclosures where they landed. As a result we have the coves of St Sennen, St Senara at Zennor, St Loy and St Levan, St Clement's Isle at Mousehole and numerous other isolated churches and holy wells. Legends tell of their adventures as they crossed the sea from Ireland to Cornwall and then to Brittany - a Celtic displacement caused by the Anglo-Saxon migrations. They built small rectangular chapels - many on the cliffs such as at St Levan near Porthcurno (3). Invariably sited near freshwater springs that were also revered in the Iron Age, some like St Levan and Madron, are still used for baptisms today. The best preserved is Madron Chapel.

Celtic Cross in Penlee Park, Penzance

Crosses

The first monuments in the sacred enclosure would have been the Celtic crosses that are so reminiscent of the Bronze Age menhirs. In fact it appears that some menhirs may well have been over carved by the early Christians.

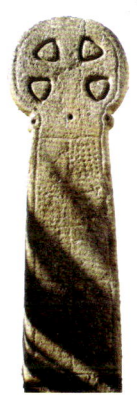

Early Christian Sites in West Cornwall

Votive offerings are still left at many Holy Wells - this is Madron

There is carving of him holding a pig above the church door. The well is known for having a strange atmosphere that freaks out some people.

St Levan Church & Chapel (3)

The church has a number of crosses (photo p31). Follow the footpath from the car park turning near the church to the coast. The well is on the cliff

Madron Well & Chapel

An important site still revered by locals and decorated with pieces of colourful rag, cloth and even plastic in the pagan fashion. The offerings are supposed to appease the spirits of the well - if you had an illness, as the cloth rotted away, so the illness went with it. The impressive remains of an early

Paul Cross (2)

In the church yard wall is a cross with a carved figure - possibly a reworking of an Iron age menhir (photo p27) - also see cross at St Buryan below.

Cross at St Buryan

Sancreed Well & Chapel

Small holy well dedicated to St.Credan, a saint who accidently killed his father and became a swineherd in penance.

St Euny's Well near to Carn Euny ancient village

top - from the well, a flight of about 50 stone steps descends to the remains of a tiny chapel where St Selevan lived. The chapel is believed to date from at least the 8th century and is one of the oldest of its kind in Cornwall.

St Euny's Well

Close to Carn Euny Village.

Sancreed Holy Well

Medieval Christian chapel lie 75m further on. The chapel still has stone benches and an altar stone. A small stream runs through the building and collects in a reservoir. Baptisms are occasionally still carried out here. Sign posted as Boswarthen Chapel off the Madron to Morvah road (take Madron turning at Heamoor roundabout on the A30 Penzance Bypass).

The remains of Sancreed chapel

This list only represents the best and most accessible sites. (6) refers to the relevant section in this book & sites shown * are on the route of the Tinner's Way.

St Michael's Mount

Mount's Bay

The towns and villages that perch on the rim of this sheltered bay - Marazion, Penzance and Newlyn - account for almost two thirds of the population of West Cornwall. The bay is a rare safe and sheltered anchorage on this coast, the next sheltered bay of any size being Falmouth on the other side of the Lizard peninsula. In the middle of the bay stands the romantic castle and former monastery of St Michael's Mount.

Fishing, farming and tourism are the major industries around the bay. Fishing is centred on Newlyn. Penzance harbour deals with small ship repair and the goods and passenger services to and from the Isles of Scilly on board the Scillonian III.

Marazion

Marazion was a thriving market town in the C10th when Penzance was just a hovel of fisherman's huts. Its prosperity was due to the large numbers of pilgrims that came here to worship at the Benedictine monastery on the Mount. It was also a point of departure for the important medieval pilgrimage route to Santiago De Compostela in Spain. Even today, the medieval harbour below St Michael's Mount is one of the largest in Cornwall although now instead of pilgrims it's visitors to the castle and gardens who make the journey to the Mount. There is a cobbled causeway at low tide with ferries at high water. Marazion has a good selection of galleries and cafes and makes a good base for families with small children.

Humphry Davy - a famous son of Penzance
keeps an eye on Market Jew Street

19

Madron & Morvah

Trengwainten Gardens

Main road to St Just

Main road to Trewidden Garden & Land's End

Newmill

Back Road to St Ives & Chysauster ancient village

B3311

Boskenwyn

Polmennor

Gulval Churchtown

B&

Treneere Roundabout

Gulval

Tesco Superstore

Heliport (Isles of Scilly 20mins)

Mount's Bay School

Heamoor

Heamoor Roundabout

A30

B3311

Ponsandane

A30

Eastern Green

Tesco Roundabout

Footbridge

Treneere

Lescudjack

Penzance

Chy-an-dour

Cycle Path on seaward side of railway

Eastern Green Beach

St Clare

Leskinnick

The Battlefields

West Cornwall Hospital

Penzance Indoor Swimming Pool & Leisure Centre

Causeway Head

Market Jew St.

Out

In

Wharfside St.

Albert Pier

LW

Western Cressar

Castle Horneck Youth Hostel

Penalverne

Police Station

Penlee Gallery

Honey Pot

Chapel St.

Morrab Rd.

HW

LW

Exchange Gallery

Boat

Lighthouse Pier

A3074

A30

Love Lane

Penlee Park

Children's play parks

Redinnick

Morrab Gdns

Carn Olven

Jubilee Outdoor Swimming Pool & Lido

Alverton

The Prom

Chimney Rocks

Battery Rocks

A30

Mount Misery Roundabout

Boating Lake

Co-op & Lidl

Wherry Town

Wherry Rocks

The Gear

Mount Misery

Newlyn Coombe

Children's play park

Tolcarne

B3315

Newlyn Green

Tolcarne Beach

Newlyn Meadery

Newlyn Gallery

Fish Mkt.

Gwavas Lake

Pedestrian ferry to the Isles of Scilly (2.5 hours)

B3315

Newlyn

Higher Faugan

Cycle Path on seaward side of road

Sandy Cove

Carn Base

Chyoone Farm

Trewarveneth

Carn Gwavas

Chyoone Grove

Penlee Quarry (disused)

Roskilly (Skilly Beach)

Low Lee Buoy

Trungle Farm

Trungle Moor

Trungle

Paul

St Michael's Mount

Tin won from the granite of West Cornwall was traded from here in Roman times and probably for hundreds of years before that. A monastery was established in the 12th century attached to Mont St Michael in Normandy. Its strategic importance led Henry VIII to make it a fortress after the Dissolution of the Monasteries in 1535. In this role it was one of the last outposts of the Royalist cause during the English Civil War - eventually falling to the Parliamentarian army in 1646. Sir John Aubyn was an officer in the Roundhead army and he became so enchanted with the Mount that he brought it from the Crown. His family still live there.

A causeway links the Mount to the mainland at low water and ferry boats operate from various small quays in Marazion depending on the state of the tide. The Castle building itself is not open every day, even in the summer, so check before you travel.

Penzance

Penzance serves the large agricultural and rural hinterland of West Cornwall and like many West Cornwall towns and villages, it has a thriving arts community and vibrant cafe life. Market Jew Street (Cornish for *Thursday market*) is a poor introduction to the town - Chapel Street is a more interesting and attractive area with pubs, restaurants and art galleries. The new Exchange Gallery - near the Egyptian House - has become a popular late night attraction with a facade that continuously changes colour. If you are interested in architecture, the area between Chapel Street and Morrab Road has a fine mix of Georgian houses.

The first settlement is thought to have been in the lee of Battery Rocks - where the harbour now stands. *Pen zance* is Cornish for *holy headland* and a small, early Christian chapel once stood on the Battery Rocks. The present St Mary's church stands proudly above the harbour and outside the south end of the

21

The fishing fleet in Newlyn harbour with Penzance in the distance

church is a rough carved figure of John the Baptist - reputedly taken from the original fisherman's chapel.

The town grew in importance as a result of its status as a stannary town, where tin from the St Just mines was assayed and traded. This lead to the establishment of banks and shops in Green Market and Market Jew Street to service the mines. The pubs in Chapel Street served to relieve the miners of their wages on pay day.

The harbour and its wet dock are always busy - the harbour gate is shut as the tide falls to keep ships afloat at low water. Small coasters and trawlers use the dry dock - as do many tenders from the naval dockyard at Devonport. The Scillonian III leaves the Lighthouse Pier, for the Isles of Scilly, in a bustle of activity at 9.15am most days in the summer and returns at about 7pm. Children love to watch the bustle of passengers, cranes and fork lift trucks. There are few better ways to finish an evening than with a stroll around the harbour or along the Promenade.

Penzance doesn't really do beaches, but this is made up for by the Jubilee Pool - a 1930's outdoor lido constructed on the Battery Rocks. Many locals like to swim from the Battery Rocks at the end of the pool.

Newlyn

The fishing industry has taken a few knocks in recent years and there is a fear that over-fishing will cause the sort of catastrophic collapse in fish stocks that saw the pilchard disappear from Cornish waters 100 years ago (see Newlyn Pilchards on p25). Even so, Newlyn still has the most valuable fish landings of any port in the country. The fish market starts about 7am and you can find almost every type of fish on sale from huge sun fish and sharks to tiny sprats. If you have time, it's worth wandering around some of the small alleys with their lovely old houses. Fishing is still a hazardous industry and there is not a year that passes without the loss of fishermen at sea. Mount Misery, above Newlyn, was where the fish wives used to anxiously gather, awaiting the return of sons, brothers and husbands from their voyages.

Pirate on the roof of the Admiral Benbow in Chapel St

Mount's Bay - places to visit

Mazey Day parade in Penzance - dressed as sweets

St Michael's Mount

Ⓟ ♛♛♛ 🍴🍵 🍽

During the season the castle is open everyday except Saturday. The gardens are open weekdays in the Spring and Thursdays & Fridays in the Summer. Guided tours and other events.
www.stmichaelsmount.co.uk
T: (01736) 710507
T: (01736) 710265 (tide & ferry)

The new extension to Newlyn Gallery overlooking The Prom

Newlyn Gallery

♿ ♛♛♛ 🚌 1,6 🍵🍽

Recently extended.
www.newlynartgallery.co.uk
T: (01736) 363715

Exchange Gallery, Pz

♿ ♛♛♛ 🍵🍽

An annex to Newlyn Art Gallery, the Exchange is a conversion of an old telephone exchange to form a modern art gallery showing international contemporary work.
www.newlynartgallery.co.uk
T: (01736) 363715

The facade of the Exchange Gallery in Penzance changes colour at night

Penlee House Gallery & Museum

Ⓟ ♿ ♛♛♛ 🍵🍽 🍽

In Penlee Park - permanent exhibitions of Newlyn School painters plus visiting art exhibitions. Displays of archaeological and historic objects from the West Cornwall area. Large children's playground in park and lovely terrace cafe.
www.penleehouse.org.uk
T: (01736) 363625

Trewidden Gardens

Ⓟ ♿ (partial) ♛♛♛ 🚌 342

Private garden with tree ferns.
www.trewiddengarden.co.uk
T: (01736) 366800

Morrab garden in the Spring

Morrab Gardens

Beautiful sub-tropical gardens in the heart of Penzance.

Trengwainton Gardens

Ⓟ ♿ (partial) ♛♛♛ 🚌 17 (Madron bus) 🍵🍽

National Trust garden containing many rare species. Lovely walled and kitchen gardens.
www.nationaltrust.org.uk
T: (01736) 363148

Penglaz dances and twirls through the streets of Penzance at Golowan

23

Things to do

Jubilee Pool

Jubilee Outdoor Pool

Wonderful surviving example of a 1930's lido with poolside cafe selling Roskilly's ice cream and jugs of sangria - it doesn't get anymore civilised than this.
T: (01736) 369224
www.jubileepool.co.uk

Penzance Indoor Pool

Modern indoor pool.

The Scillonian III

Boat Trips

Fishing and coastal cruises, fast rib rides - tickets from the Shell Shop and old RNLI office at the harbour.

Day Trip to Tresco

Take the helicopter to Tresco, Isles of Scilly to see the wonderful sub-tropical gardens.
T: 01736 363871
www.islesofscillyhelicopter.com

Swim off Battery Rocks

Join the locals who swim in the sea at the end of the Battery rocks by Jubilee Pool.

Cycle to Mousehole or Marazion

There are good off-road cycle paths from Penzance to Marazion and Mousehole. Cycle Hire at The Wharfside Centre or at Penzance Cycles.

Golowan - Mazey Day & Montol

Golowan is a Celtic festival of midsummer, celebrated on the feast of St John the Baptist at the end of June each year. Penglaz (a snapping horse skull on a stick) is the Penzance 'Obby 'Oss that dances through the street from dawn to dusk goaded on by the Golowan Band. There are parades through the streets and Mazey Day (Saturday) is preceded by a week of music, poetry and arts events. Montol is the midwinter solstice in November.
www.golowan.org

Train trip to St Ives

Only a total fool would drive to St Ives in the school summer holidays - instead take the spectacular train trip as the railway follows St Ives Bay.

St Mary's Church in Chapel Street

Eating Out

For families there is a meadery at the harbour and one at Newlyn. Chapel Street has lots of restaurants - also try the Smugglers in Newlyn.

Treat Yourself....

at the Honey Pot Cafe.

If you do just one thing....

come to Mazey Day.

Treat yourself - The Honey Pot cafe near Chapel Street Co-op

Newlyn Pilchards & Painters

You can gauge from this photograph the huge catch to be had and the collective effort required to land the shoals

Newlyn Pilchards

The arrival of the pilchard in the spring was once the herald of frantic activity in Cornwall. Every small village and settlement along the coast could land millions of fish. Every conceivable container would be brought into action to salt the fish before they went off. This was often done in open courtyard buildings called pilchard palaces, which you can still make out in Newlyn, Mousehole, Penberth, Sennen, Treen Cove (Gurnard's Head) and St Ives. As the mounds of fish were stacked higher and higher between layers of salt the fish would be said to 'sigh' as their swim bladders ruptured giving an eerie serenade to the smelly work. The oil was collected in gullies and used in lamps. When most of

"The Pilchard Works" Newlyn, Cornwall

Newlyn 1901 by Walter Langley

the oil had been extracted, the fish were salted and packed in barrels for export to the Mediterranean. Salted fish is a popular dish for Catholic families because of the tradition of not eating red meat on Fridays. Apparently the smell was appalling. Fortunately, those who worked here on a regular basis seemed to acquire an immunity - however the pilchard palaces soon became know as the stinking palaces. Pilchard fishing rivalled tin mining as an industry in the C19th and the trade still survives in the West Cornwall at the Pilchard Works in Newlyn. The pilchard shoals migrated north in the Spring and Summer to the North Atlantic and North Sea. Their usual behaviour was to hug the coastline and swim near the surface, where they fed on rich plankton released by

coastal shellfish. This pattern of behaviour was successful for thousands of years and supported massive numbers of fish. Unfortunately in the C18th and C19th it proved to be the undoing of the species. The huge shoals were easily spotted from the cliffs and specially posted watchers would then direct the village boats to the right place. The surrounded fish would take up the shape of a protective ball - this only eased their demise. The stocks became exhausted and the shoals disappeared before the First World War, never to return in the same numbers.

Where to buy

Cornish pilchards are on sale at Waitrose, Trelawney Fish in Newlyn (opposite the inshore lifeboat house) and Lavender's deli in Penzance.
www.pilchardworks.co.uk

Typical pilchard palace with its huge stack of pilchards

Newlyn Painters

The Newlyn Gallery was set up to exhibit the work of the Newlyn Society of Artists who established a colony in West Cornwall in the late C19th and early C20th. They left a wonderful record of the fishing industry and the people that worked in it. Many of their best works can now be seen at Penlee House Gallery in Penzance.

Walter Langley was one of the first artists to move to Penzance - he arrived in 1882 and painted many of the most recognisable works of the New-

In a Cornish Fishing Village, Departure of the Fleet for the North - Walter Langley

Perhaps the most famous painter of the group was Stanhope Forbes. He was influenced by the French 'plein air' painters and, to the end of his long life, was often to be found painting away on the cliffs.

Forbes originally moved to Newlyn in 1884. In 1899 he founded a school of painting with his wife, Elizabeth Forbes. Elizabeth painted the gorgeous 'A Zandvoort Fishergirl'. Together they helped to bring on a new generation of artists such as Harold Harvey, Laura and Harold Knight and this helped to prompt a second flowering of work in the 1920's and 1930's.

Many of this generation of painters lived in the Lamorna Valley, and became known as the Lamorna Group led by Samuel 'Lamorna' Birch who lived above the tiny harbour.

Art Pass

The Art Pass offers seven day unlimited access to six West Cornwall galleries - Tate St Ives, Barbara Hepworth Museum and Sculpture Garden, Leach Pottery, Penlee House Gallery & Museum, and Newlyn Art Gallery & the Exchange.

Cornish Line-caught mackerel fillets
in lemon and basil marinade

Penlee House

www.penleehouse.org.uk
T: (01736) 363625

The Sunny South - Walter Langley 1885

lyn School - often watercolours painted in great detail illustrating scenes from the day-to-day life of the community.

Norman Garstin came to Penzance in 1889 and painted one of the most loved pictures in the Penlee Collection - 'The Rain it Raineth Every Day' - a view of a windblown and wave swept Penzance Prom.

The Rain it Raineth Every Day - Norman Garstin 1889

Two of the old granite quarries above Lamorna Cove

Mousehole, Lamorna and St Loy, are sheltered from the worst of the south-westerly gales and also have the advantage of south facing slopes that concentrate the warmth of the sun. As a consequence, the cliffs from Mousehole to Merthen Point are covered in tiny fields once used to grow early daffodils, violets and lilies for the London market. The fields have long since been left to run wild but many varieties have become naturalised on the cliff top.

Mousehole

One of the prettiest villages in Cornwall and now well known as the home of the Mousehole Cat. The Mousehole itself is a large cave to the west of the harbour. Houses, craft shops, cafes and art galleries crowd around the tiny harbour. The village with its narrow streets is difficult to negotiate in a car even in midwinter. There is a large car park and roadside parking on the Penzance side of the village or consider getting the bus from Penzance. If your Christmas spirit is flagging and jaded then the lights at Mousehole will put you right. People travel from all over to the world to see the Christmas lights that illuminate the harbour and hillside. Tom Bawcock's Eve is held on the night before Christmas Eve and celebrates his saving the village from starvation. Star-gazey pie - a pie with whole baked fish with their heads poking out of the crust - is served at the Ship and there is much singing of Cornish carols, parades of lanterns and drinking. The Sea Salts & Sail Festival of traditional working boats is held every 2 years in July.

Cross at Paul Church - possibly a Christian reworking of an ancient menhir

27

Lamorna

A favourite place for artists from the Newlyn School of post-impressionist painters. Lamorna Birch, Laura Knight and Dod Proctor formed the Lamorna Group in the first half of the C20th. Some of their work can been seen in Penlee Gallery in Penzance. The granite quarries on either side of the small harbour and at Castallack, are now rather beautifully overgrown. The spoil heaps show just how much stone had to be excavated to produce workable blocks. The granite has unusually large quartz crystals - it was used, and can be seen in many of the buildings of Penzance.

St Loy's Cove

The Merry Maidens

In this small area there are archaeological remains from the Stone, Bronze and Iron Ages. Despite their very different ages, they appear to be part of one large arrangement based around the Merry Maidens circle. The oldest structure is the Stone Age Tregiffian Barrow - it's at least 4,000 years old. Inside the chamber is a carved, pitted stone that seems to echo the

eroded stones on the top of many natural carns. Folklore often associates this sort of stone with druids, who were supposed to have used them to catch blood from sacrifices. The floor of the tomb has yielded the

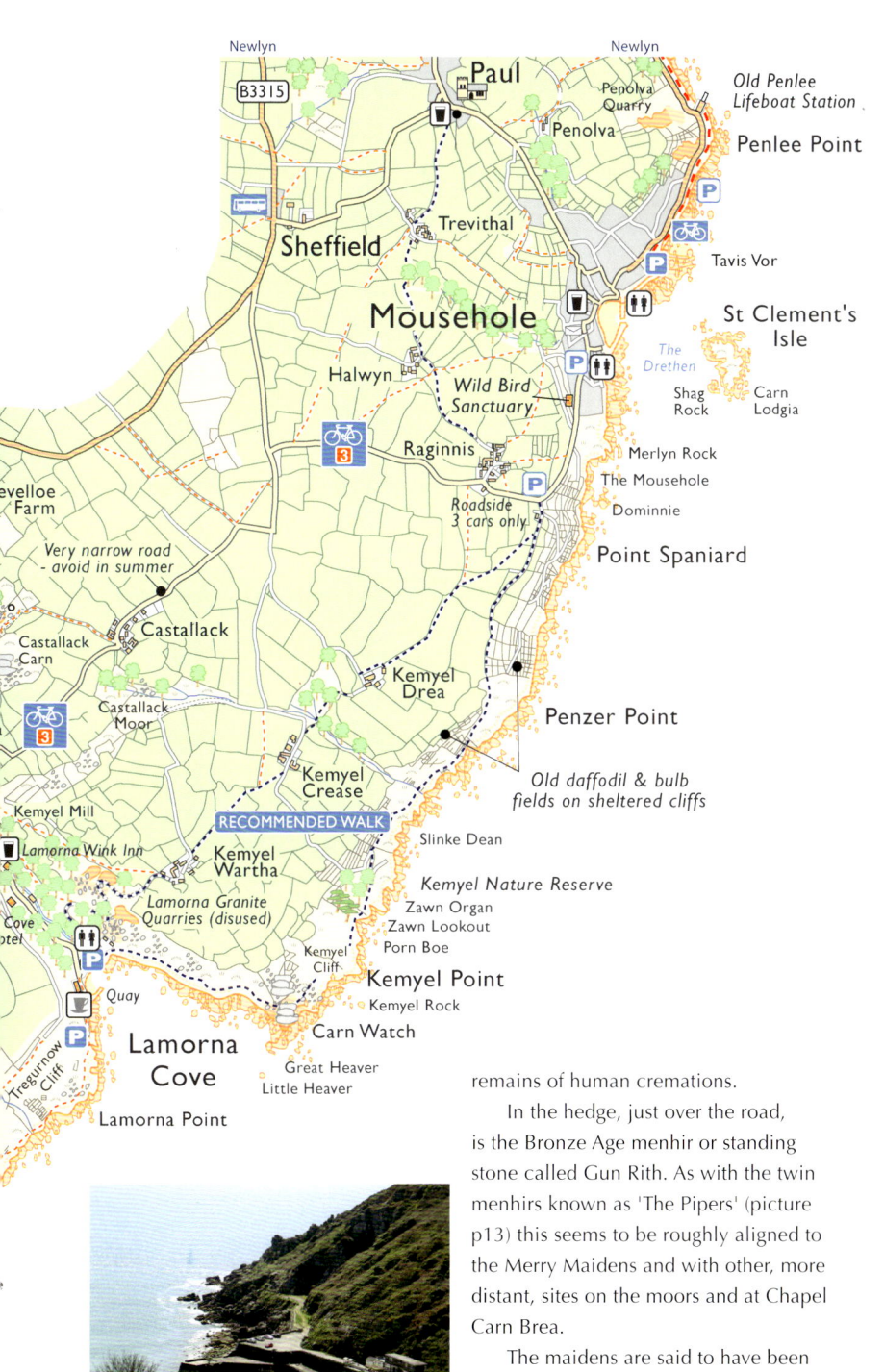

Newlyn Newlyn

Paul

B3315

Penolva Quarry

Old Penlee Lifeboat Station

Penolva

Penlee Point

Trevithal

Tavis Vor

Sheffield

St Clement's Isle

Mousehole

The Drethen

Halwyn

Shag Rock Carn Lodgia

Wild Bird Sanctuary

Merlyn Rock
The Mousehole

Raginnis

Dominnie

Roadside 3 cars only

Point Spaniard

evelloe Farm

Very narrow road - avoid in summer

Castallack

Castallack Carn

Kemyel Drea

Penzer Point

Castallack Moor

Old daffodil & bulb fields on sheltered cliffs

Kemyel Crease

Kemyel Mill

Lamorna Wink Inn

RECOMMENDED WALK

Slinke Dean

Kemyel Wartha

Kemyel Nature Reserve

Lamorna Granite Quarries (disused)

Zawn Organ
Zawn Lookout
Porn Boe

Cove otel

Kemyel Cliff

Kemyel Point

Quay

Kemyel Rock

Carn Watch

Lamorna Cove

Great Heaver
Little Heaver

Tregurnow Cliff

Lamorna Point

remains of human cremations.

In the hedge, just over the road, is the Bronze Age menhir or standing stone called Gun Rith. As with the twin menhirs known as 'The Pipers' (picture p13) this seems to be roughly aligned to the Merry Maidens and with other, more distant, sites on the moors and at Chapel Carn Brea.

The maidens are said to have been turned to stone for dancing on the Sabbath - a fate that also befell the Pipers who provided the accompaniment.

Lamorna Cove

29

Recommended walks around Lamorna and Mousehole

St Loy Woods

St Loy Woods & Cove

Ⓟ (very limited) 👫

This is a really good walk for children as there are streams to cross and plenty of trees to climb. St Loy's Cove is a granite boulder beach - so it's not possible to swim from here. The best times to visit are March and May when the woods are blanketed first with daffodils and then bluebells. Take your wellies as the paths can be very muddy after rain. From the road, follow the stream down to the valley and after you cross the stream and climb up the side of the valley to meet the coast path, take the stile on your left and climb back down towards the cove on the coast path.

Distance: 2km/1.25 miles round trip (1 hour).

Parking: Roadside parking for 3 cars at the top of the path just before the bridge. The local farmer allows parking in his field just past Trevedran Farm in the busy summer months.

Going: Generally OK, one steep climb down to cove at the coast path.

Pub/Refreshments: at Lamorna Pottery.

Mousehole to Lamorna

Ⓟ 👫 🚻 🍷 🍴

This is part of a traditional Easter walk from Newlyn and Mousehole to Lamorna. The first part follows the inland path and then drops into Lamorna Valley past the old granite quarries. After stopping at the Lamorna Wink for food and drink the return is along the coast path. I suggest you park at Paul and walk from there as Mousehole and Lamorna have limited parking in the summer months.

Distance: 5km/3 miles round trip (3 hours not including pub time).

Parking: at Lamorna Cove or in Mousehole (steep walk to

Lamorna Valley

reach footpath) or roadside parking for 2 cars at the corner below Raginnis. Alternatively start from Paul village above Mousehole - there is a car park next to the King's Head pub. You could take the bus to Lamorna from Penzance and walk back towards Mousehole where you can pick up a frequent bus service back to Newlyn and Penzance.

Going: Generally OK ,the section from Lamorna to Kemyel Cliff involves scrambling over some cliff top boulders.

Pub/Refreshments: Cafes at Lamorna Cove, Lamorna Pottery and in Mousehole. The Lamorna Wink pub does a good crab sandwich. Mousehole has cafes and shops.

Places to Visit

Mousehole Wild Bird Hospital

Set up by the Yglesias sisters in 1928 and famous following the Torrey Canyon oil tanker wreck in 1967. Cares for injured and oiled birds - still going strong. www.mouseholebirdhospital.org.uk

Lamorna Pottery

Ⓟ ♿ 👫 🚻 🍷 🍴

Set in the woods at Lamorna Turning - lovely setting, cream teas, dinners and craft shop.

Things to Do

Sea Salts & Sail

Festival of traditional boats and crafts held every two years in July since 1996 - fish smoking,

crab pot making and lots more. www.seasalts.co.uk

If you do just one thing....come to the Xmas lights at Mousehole.

Eating Out

Mousehole has restaurants - the views from the Old Coastguard Hotel are particularly good - garden for kids too.

3. Logan Rock, Porthcurno & Gwennap Head

Pedn beach with Treryn Dinas and Logan Rock behind

In this section we start the transition away from the sheltered cliffs and wooded valleys of the south coast towards the more exposed western cliffs. I cannot think of any more beautiful parts of the this coast than this section between Treryn Dinas and Gwennap Head. The soft sandy beaches at Porthcurno and Pedn Vounder can't be bettered anywhere in Cornwall. This is a very dramatic and interesting part of the coastline - the local archaeology and wildlife could almost fill a book by themselves.

Penberth Cove

Penberth Cove still has a number of small boats fishing from the slip - mostly for crab, lobster and mackerel. The building on the foreshore was once a pilchard palace (see Newlyn Pilchards).

St Levan's Church

Beautifully sited church undoubtedly standing on a very ancient site. St Levan himself is thought to have landed at Porth Chapel. The great fissured stone in the churchyard was a favourite resting place of St Levan. He broke the stone with his staff and legend says that the world will end when a donkey with loaded panniers can pass through the fissure. The stone crosses in the churchyard probably marked the original holy enclosure before a church was ever built here. Two other Celtic crosses are found within a few hundred metres marking the paths that radiate from the church. The churchyard holds some of the graves of victims of the Khyber, wrecked at Porth Loe in 1904.

Cross at St Levan Church

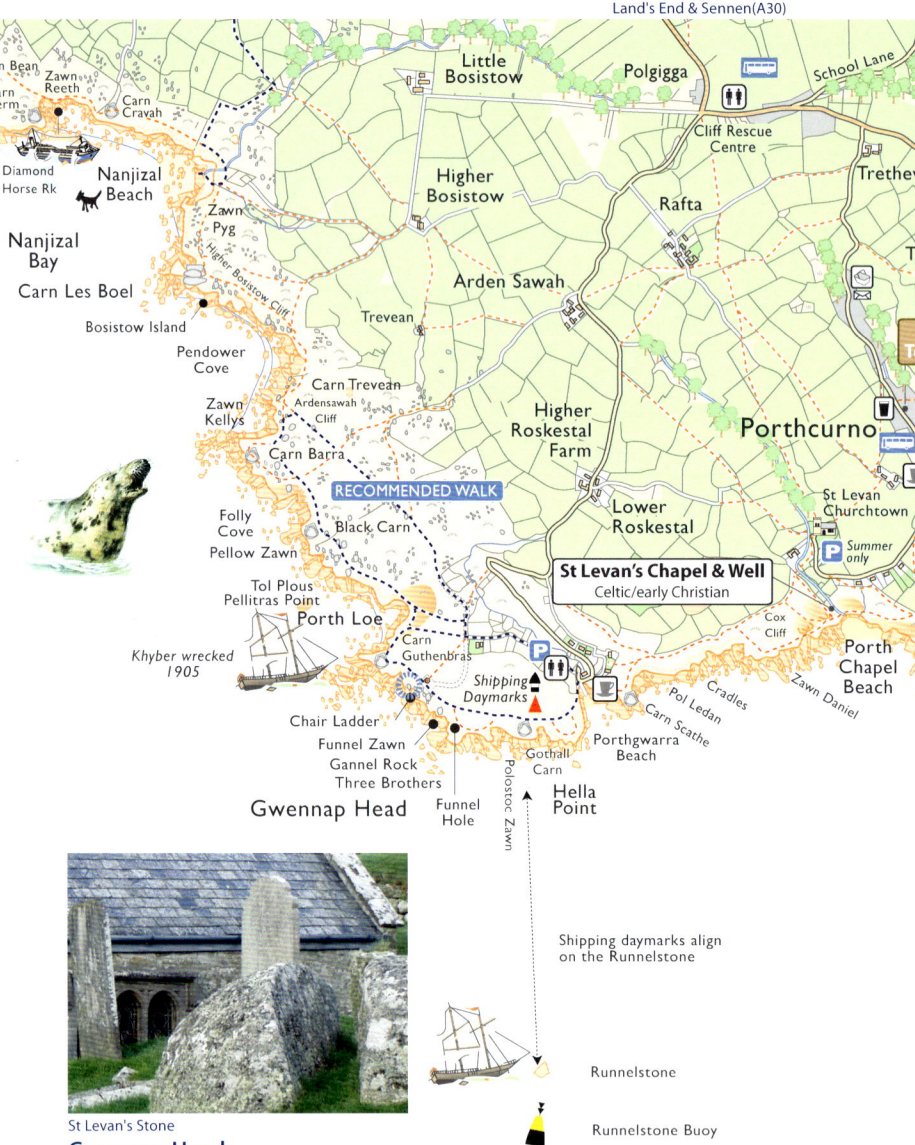

Little Bosistow
Polgigga
School Lane

rn Bean
Zawn Reeth
Carn Cravah

Diamond Horse Rk
Nanjizal Beach

Higher Bosistow

Cliff Rescue Centre

Trethewe

Zawn Pyg

Nanjizal Bay

Carn Les Boel

Rafta

Tre

Higher Bostow Cliff

Bosistow Island

Arden Sawah

Pendower Cove

Trevean

Porthcurno

Tele

Zawn Kellys

Carn Trevean
Ardensawah Cliff

Higher Roskestal Farm

St Levan Churchtown

Carn Barra

RECOMMENDED WALK

Lower Roskestal

Porthcurno

Summer only

Folly Cove
Pellow Zawn

Black Carn

St Levan's Chapel & Well
Celtic/early Christian

Cox Cliff

Tol Plous
Pellitras Point

Porth Loe

Carn Guthenbras

Porth Chapel Beach

Khyber wrecked 1905

Shipping Daymarks

Cradles

Zawn Daniel

Pol Ledan

Carn Scathe

Chair Ladder

Funnel Zawn
Gannel Rock
Three Brothers

Porthgwarra Beach

Gothall Carn

Gwennap Head

Funnel Hole

Hella Point

Polostoc Zawn

Shipping daymarks align on the Runnelstone

St Levan's Stone

Runnelstone

Runnelstone Buoy

Gwennap Head

The fisherman's Land's End. The sea is always a swirling confusion here as the tides from the Bristol and English Channel meet and mix. Look to the south west and you can see the lonely Wolf Rock Lighthouse sitting on the pinnacle of an ancient volcano and further away, to the west, the Isles of Scilly can be made out on a clear day. Get a pasty from the little shop at Porthgwarra.

St Levan's Well & Porthchapel

The holy well is attributed with magical powers and is said to be particularly effective in curing tooth and eye complaints. It is still used for baptisms. St Levan, in common with many Cornish saints, lived as a hermit. The foundations of his small cell are visible on the cliff below the well.

Map labels

St Buryan

Trevedran

B3315

Silena Farm

Treverven House

In field (summer only)

Penberth Valley

Burnewhall Farm

Treverven Farm

St Lo[y]

Boscean

Logan Rock

Penberth

Penguarnon

Porthguarnon Cove

Treen

Roadside

The Pulpit

Le Scathe Cove

Gazells

Coffin Rock

[P]churno [o]h Museum

RECOMMENDED WALK

Cove Farm

Penberth Cove

Me

Treen Cliff

Castle Ramparts

Carn Kizzie

Kite's Carn

Cribba Head

Pedn Vounder Beach

Hall Dinas

Polpy Cove

The Logan Rock

Porthcurno Beach

Seghy

The Minack
Cliff theatre & visitor centre

Treryn Dinas

Treryn Dinas Castle
Iron Age Cliff Castle

[-]men-an-mere
or
[W]ireless Point

Under sea telephone cables
Trans Globe fibre optic link

Minack Theatre with Treryn Dinas in the background

Porthcurno & Minack Theatre

Hidden beneath the soft shell sand of the beach are numerous trans-ocean communication cables - Porthcurno is the first suitable landing place in the UK. The cables were considered so important that during the Second World War tin miners were drafted in to hew out bomb-proof chambers in the granite cliffs. The chambers are now part of Porthcurno Museum of Telegraphy.

The Minack Theatre is cut into the cliffs south of the beach. This open air theatre is the setting for plays during the summer. There is a cliff top cafe and an exhibition on the remarkable lady who created the theatre. Even the famous Greek amphitheatre's of antiquity would find it hard to match the grand backdrop of the sea and setting sun. There are matinee and evening performances. It is quite unforgettable to watch a performance of Romeo and Juliet and have Romeo speaking to the real moon as it rises above the Logan Rock. Don't forget to take a picnic and plenty of cushions and rugs.

Recommended Walks around Porthcurno

Treryn Dinas & the Logan Rock

Ⓟ (at Treen)

This wonderful cliff walk starts from Treen but could equally be done from Penberth or Porthcurno. It combines many of the elements that make West Cornwall special - the ancient history; the intense beauty of the beaches all set against the granite cliffs. Look out for gorse covered in mats of pink threads - this is dodder - an unusual parasitic plant. Treryn Dinas is one of the best preserved Iron Age cliff castles in Cornwall. The headland is an obvious defensive site with only the landward side needing man-made defences. The high earth ramparts would

The Logan Rock

probably have been surmounted with a wooden palisade. It's not thought that the site was a permanent settlement because it's so exposed plus it has no fresh water supply. Perhaps it would have been the Iron Age equivalent of an air raid shelter used in times of imminent danger from raiding Irishmen and Norsemen. Inside the cliff castle, on top of the second large granite outcrop, is a *logan* or *rocking* stone. Common throughout Cornwall on the tops of granite carns these naturally occurring stones sit on a tiny point of contact with the rock beneath. It's possible for a child to rock a block of granite weighing many tons backwards and forwards. This stone does not move much. It

Parasitic dodder on gorse

was levered out of place by a Lt. Goldsmith of HMS Nimble in 1824 as a bet. The locals were outraged, the Admiralty forced him to erect an elaborate pulley mechanism to retrieve the rock and place it back in its original position - all at his own expense.

Distance: 2 km/1.25 miles round trip (1 hour).

Parking: Car park at Treen, limited roadside parking at Penberth - best avoided in busy summer months.

Going: OK - when inside the cliff castle follow the path on eastern side of the headland to get to the top of the outcrop. Probably a bit scary for small children.

Pub/Refreshments: Logan Rock pub and cafe in Treen.

Places to Visit

Minack Theatre

Ⓟ ♿ ⋔ ♨ ☕

Afternoon and evening plays. Visitor centre during the day. Cafe has spectacular views. www.minack.com
T: (01736) 810181/810471

Gwennap Head

Seals breed in the caves below Gwennap Head and Pendower Cove - you'll need binoculars.

Porthcurno Museum of Telegraphy

Ⓟ ♿ ⋔ ♨ ☕

Porthcurno is an important part of the undersea telcom cable network. Visit the underground tunnels build to protect the station during WW2.

www.porthcurno.org.uk
T: (01736) 810 966

Eating Out

Logan Rock Inn at Treen.

Treat Yourself....

to a cup of tea at the Minack Cafe - espresso with a view.

If you do just one thing....

swim at Pedn.

4. Land's End & Sennen

Gamper Bay

The cliffs and coast around Land's End, and the wide beaches at Sennen and Gwynver, are the most popular places in West Cornwall during the summer months. The cliffs offer great walking, especially in the evenings as the sun drops down behind Longships Lighthouse and the Isles of Scilly. At the same time locals get their barbecues out at Sennen after a day of swimming and surfing. Look out for the rare atmospheric phenomenon of 'green flash' just as the sun dips below the horizon.

Nanjizal Bay

This peaceful, sandy cove is never busy and is always worth exploring. You can swim in the pool below the huge rock arch on the east of the beach. Stroll down to Nanjizal through Trevilley hamlet and across the fields.

Land's End

Despite its fame, popularity and development, Land's End has lost little of its attraction - its situation is simply too impressive. This is particularly true when there is a strong sea running and waves are crashing over Longships Lighthouse, just off-shore. There are displays and information on the history and wildlife of this part of the coast. Children will enjoy a visit to pet the animals at Carn Greeb Farm. Birdwatchers flock to this area during the spring and autumn migrations when the sky becomes a Piccadilly Circus of migrating birds. Dollar Cove is the scene of a recently rediscovered wreck, thought to contain millions of pounds worth of Spanish gold and silver *macuquinas*. A wobbly steel wire bridge crosses over the Cove.

Longships lighthouse at Land's End

Longships Lighthouse

The first lighthouse here was commissioned in 1794 and did a manful job in a desperately exposed site. However it was never really high enough and was often swamped in rough seas, reducing the visibility of the light to passing ships. The present granite lighthouse was started in 1870 and was manned until 1988. The keepers took watch in shifts and their families lived in the row of houses at Land's End. The lighthouse is now fully automated with fuel for the generators being delivered to the helipad on the top of the lighthouse.

Whitesand Ba

Little Bo
Bo Cowloe

The Tribber

Shark's Fin

Pedn-men-du

Irish Lady Rk

Mayon Cliff
Bronze Age burial mound

Castle Zaw

Gamper
Bay

Maen Cliff Castle
Iron Age cliff castle

Gamper
Hole

Carn
Clo

Fillis

Kettle's Bottom

Dr Syntax's Head

Land's End

Maenek

Longships Lighthouse

Dollar Cove

Land's End
Theme Par

Carn Bras

Tal-y-maen

Dr Johnson's Head

P

Greeb Zawn

Carn
Greeb

The Armed Knight

Enys Dodman

Zawn Wells

Pordenack Point

Lion's Den

Zawr

Guillemots & Razorbills breed
on The Armed Knight

Ca

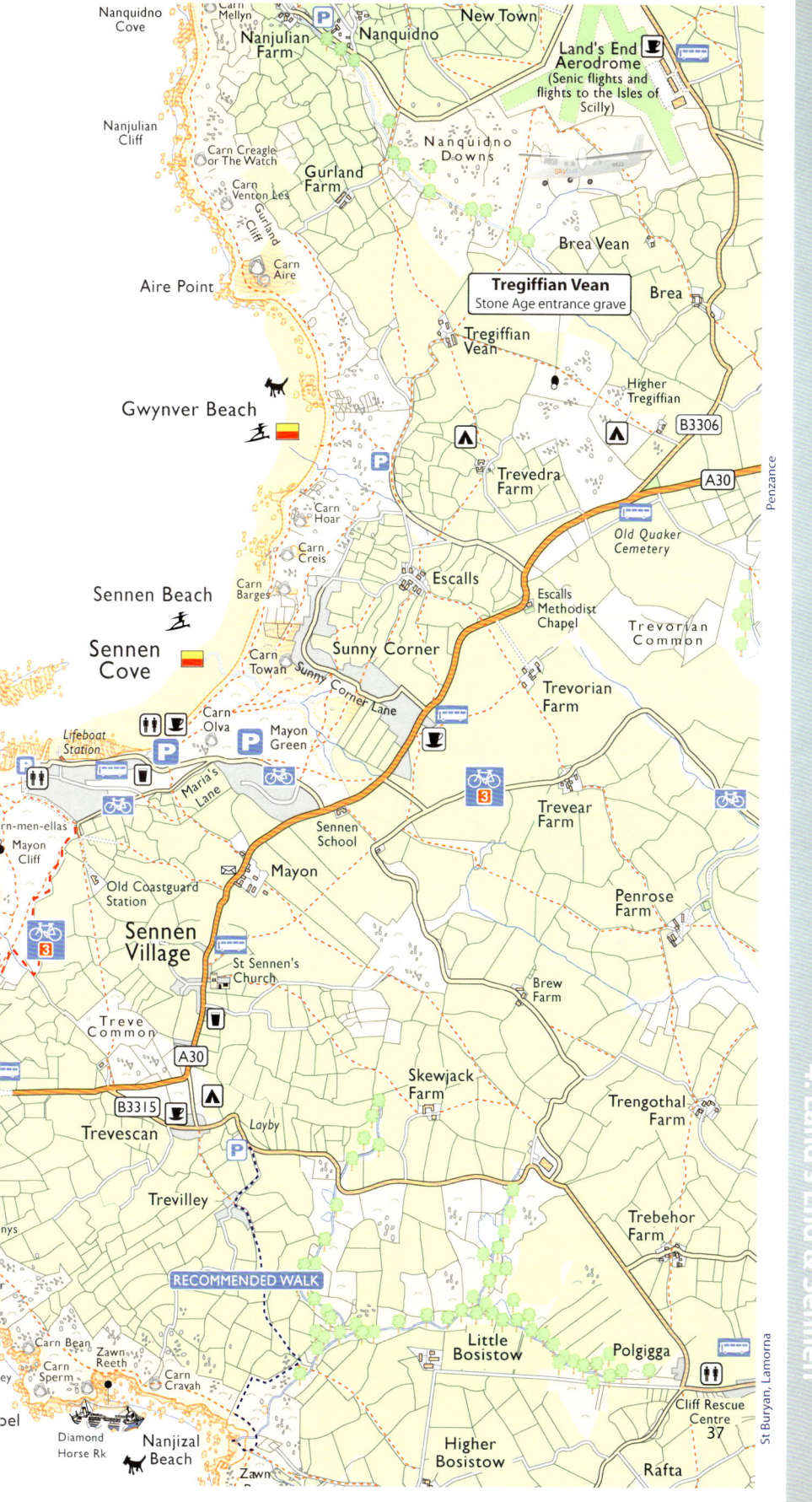

Nanquidno
Cove

Carn
Mellyn

Nanjulian
Farm

New Town

Nanquidno

Land's End
Aerodrome
(Scenic flights and
flights to the Isles of
Scilly)

Nanjulian
Cliff

Carn Creagle
or The Watch

Carn
Venton Les

Gurland
Farm

Nanquidno
Downs

Brea Vean

Brea

Gurland
Cliff

Aire Point

Carn
Aire

Tregiffian Vean
Stone Age entrance grave

Tregiffian
Vean

Higher
Tregiffian

B3306

Gwynver Beach

A30

Penzance

Carn
Hoar

Trevedra
Farm

Old Quaker
Cemetery

Carn
Creis

Escalls

Trevorian
Common

Sennen Beach

Carn
Barges

Escalls
Methodist
Chapel

Sennen
Cove

Carn
Towan

Sunny Corner

Trevorian
Farm

Carn
Olva

Sunny Corner Lane

Lifeboat
Station

Mayon
Green

Trevear
Farm

Maria's
Lane

Sennen
School

rn-men-ellas

Penrose
Farm

Mayon
Cliff

Mayon

Old Coastguard
Station

Brew
Farm

Sennen
Village

St Sennen's
Church

Treve
Common

Skewjack
Farm

Trengothal
Farm

A30

B3315

Layby

Trevescan

Trebehor
Farm

Trevilley

RECOMMENDED WALK

Carn Bean

Zawn
Reeth

Carn
o' Sperm

Little
Bosistow

Polgigga

Carn
Cravah

Cliff Rescue
Centre
37

St Buryan, Lamorna

Diamond
Horse Rk

Nanjizal
Beach

Higher
Bosistow

Rafta

Zawn

Wreck of the Mulheim at Mayon Cliff in 2003

The Wolf Rock Lighthouse

One of the most exposed lighthouses in the British Isles. It is said that the rock is called the Wolf because of the howling noise caused by high winds as they are forced between the walls of a cleft in the rock. The first lighthouse took seven years to build and was finished in 1862 after all earlier attempts were destroyed by the first winter storms. Waves frequently break over the top of the 35m tower in storms. This drove one of the first, solitary keepers mad with fear and led to the rule that there should be at least two keepers on the lighthouse at any one time. It is now fully automated with a helicopter platform for maintenance and fuel deliveries.

Sennen Cove

The most popular beach in West Cornwall with over a mile of sand. The granite rocks vary tremendously in texture and colour which makes for delightful rock pools.

Gwynver Beach

The steep climb down from the small cliff top car park make this a less busy beach than Sennen and its particularly popular with surfers. Get here early to get a space in the small car park.

A macuquinas or rough cut Spanish colonial silver dollar. It depicts the pillars of Hercules - the portal created by Hercules when he clubbed the Atlas mountains apart to make the Atlantic and Mediterranean seas. It was originally symbolic of the of the limits the known world but was adapted by the Conquistadors to become a portal to the unknown on their voyages of discovery for gold, silver and riches in the New World. The inscription between the pillars reads PLVS VLTR (plus ultra) - 'more beyond'. Thousands of silver and gold coins like this were reputedly lost into the sea in the area of Dollar Cove from wrecked Spanish ships. Keep your eyes open on the beach - you never know...

Places to Visit

Land's End

Ⓟ ♿ ⭍ 🚻 🚽 🍽

Always fun and set in magnificent location. The Isles of Scilly are visible in the west. Lots for children to do.
www.landsend-landmark.co.uk

Things to Do

Surf school for all ages

Sennen Surfing Centre
www.sennensurfingcentre.com
T: (01736) 871227
SurfSmart School www.bluelagoonsurf.com
T: (01736) 871 817

Evening fireworks at Land's End

Tuesday and Thursdays in the summer school holidays at dusk - magical.

Land's End Airport

Charter fights and trips to the Isles of Scilly.

Eating Out

The Beach at Sennen
T: (01736) 871191

Treat Yourself....to fish & chips at Sennen.

If you do to just one thing....evening barbecue on Sennen beach.

5. Mining in West Cornwall - a modern underworld

Levant Mine still has a working steam engine

Almost every part of the cliffs and moors between Cape Cornwall and Pendeen have been mined for tin and copper, often several times over as new technology allowed lower and lower concentrations of metal to be recovered. With the exception of the high ground around Ding Dong, the ore becomes richer further out to sea and less concentrated further inland. The miners, in their rapacious quest for ore even extended the galleries under the sea - sometimes with fatal consequences as the sea broke in and flooded the workings.

Centuries of mining from the Bronze Age to the end of the C20th have created a strange landscape of spoil heaps and ruins and a network of voids and galleries under-

ground. Mine engine houses that were used for pumping, lifting and crushing the ore have taken on a curious ruined grandeur.

Tin and copper ore in West Cornwall occur in unusually concentrated veins or lodes. In this area they strike the coast at right angle and The ore is sometimes as much as 10% pure metal as opposed

to the less than 1% found in alluvial deposits elsewhere in the world. It is this high concentration of metal that has made it economic to mine ore in the hard rock and under the difficult conditions found in West Cornwall. The lodes tend to occur as near vertical sheets within the surrounding rock, often only 30cm wide. Where the lodes outcrop on the

The Crowns Mine near Botallack

A typical mined out ore load in Rosevale mine. The timber props are considered to be safer because they 'whisper' or creak when they are about to collapse whereas the pillars of ore can collapse without warning

was first used by the Bronze Age people to make farming implements and weapons - bronze is an alloy of tin and copper. Bronze Age swords and spears dating back 3,000 years can be seen at Penlee House Museum in Penzance and at the Royal Cornwall Museum in Truro. There is also evidence to suggest that copper and tin ingots were being exported from St Michael's Mount to the Mediterranean 2,000 years ago. This must have been a lucrative trade, perhaps help-ing to finance the building of the bijoux Iron Age courtyard houses at Chysauster overlook-ing the bay.

As the sources of stream tin became exhausted in the C10th miners started to dig out the lodes from the solid rock by enlarging the natural zawns and also working from above to form deep gullies or *coffins*. At this time there where two natural limits on the mining of tin and copper. Firstly, the ore and the surrounding rock was simply so hard that contempo-rary tools had trouble breaking it up. Secondly, as the workings reached the water table they soon became flooded. The problem of flooding was

The adits that drain mine water on to many beaches in West Cornwall echo the Celtic holy springs believed to lead to the underworld

solved to some extent by driving tunnels or adits in from the cliff base allowing water to flow out to the sea and thereby lowering the water table. It was not until the early C19th that the new technology of steam driven pumps allowed the mines to be worked below the water table for the first time - the pumps drawing water up to the level of the adit to be drained away. Coupled with the timely invention of dynamite the mines rapidly expanded, reaching depths of over 1,000 feet 'below adit' and extending outwards under the sea. At Levant Mine the under-sea galleries were worked to within a few feet of the seabed. It is said that during storms the rumble of boulders being thrown along the seabed could be heard in the mine galleries below.

cliffs the sea exploits the join between the lode and the rock to erode deep gullies locally known as zawns. Many of the early lodes must have been discovered by following the line of the zawns or by locating the green copper verdigris that weeps from the lodes where they are exposed to the atmosphere.

The mineral lodes have also been weathered by wind and rain over tens of thou-sands of years from above, so that the heavier tin ore is found in naturally graded concentra-tions within the beds of local streams. It was probably this easily won stream tin that

An unusually horizontal seam or 'load' in Rosevale Mine. The roof is supported on timber posts with sections of ore also left in place. The concentration of copper in the ore can be gauged by the copper verdigris 'weeping out of the rock'

Carn Galva mine

The miners worked on a self employed basis, bidding against one another to work a set lode for the owner and taking a proportion of the profit. The competitive nature of the bidding for lodes and the independence of spirit of the miners themselves, worked against the organisation of the miners into unions that might have improved conditions. Working in the cramped and narrow lodes was hard with constant dampness and intense heat given off by the surrounding rocks. The average life expectancy of a miner was less than 40 years.

Fortunes were made as production in the mines peaked in the middle of the C19th. Foremost in this area where the Bolitho family who own Trengwainton House near Penzance and are still large landowners. At one time they owned a bank, a smelting works as well as a number of mines.

The good times could not last forever and the tin price collapsed in the 1880's as new, cheaper, overseas alluvial tin swamped the market and many miners were forced to emigrate. They found work in the diamond and gold mines of Canada, Mexico, South Africa and Australia. To this day there are still strong family links.

Geevor was the last mine in West Cornwall, it finally closed in 1993 ending 3,000 years of continuous mining industry. The visible remains of the mines are mostly on the surface - the engine houses such as The Crowns near Botallack perched on the edge of the cliff and the spoil dumps which are now slowly being reclaimed by plants and animals to create a new habitat.

The Crowns engine houses - part of Botallack Mine

Best Mining Sites to Visit

Levant Engine House

Ⓟ ♿ 👨‍👩‍👦

Perched on the edge of a cliff, this is the only working, steam driven, mine pumping engine left in Cornwall. Next to Geevor. www.nationaltrust.org.uk and navigate to Levant Mine for 'steaming' times.

Geevor Tin Mine Museum

Ⓟ ♿ 👨‍👩‍👦 🚌 🍴 👫

Geevor was the last working tin mine in West Cornwall. There are tours of the surface and underground workings - a must for those interested in the mining history of the area. Shop, cafe and information. The shop has a large selection of books on the history of mining in the area.
T: (01736) 788662
www.geevor.com

Wayside Museum, Zennor

Ⓟ ♿ 👨‍👩‍👦 🚌 🍴 👫

Small and intimate award winning museum, illustrating the life of local working people in the last century.

Cot Valley, St Just

Ⓟ (at the bottom of the valley) 👨‍👩‍👦 🚌

Plenty to see in this valley where water mills helped concentrate the tin ore. Also good for bird watching.

Botallack Count House

Ⓟ 👨‍👩‍👦 🚌

Impressive arsenic calciners - used to collect valuable arsenic from the tin ore.

Crowns Engine Houses

Ⓟ 👨‍👩‍👦 🚌

Park at the Count House in Botallack and walk down the cliff - spectacular.

Rosevale Mine, Zennor

👨‍👩‍👦 🚌

Private mine that runs guided tours of the underground workings for groups of 5 or more - see photos on previous page. Involves climbing ladders and squeezing through small openings. Not for small children, but as close as you will ever get to experiencing what it was like underground in a small West Cornwall mine. Tours take 1-2 hours. Safety helmets and equipment are provided and you will need boots and waterproof clothing. www.rosevalemine.co.uk

6. St Just, Cape Cornwall & Pendeen

![Cape Cornwall]

Cape Cornwall

This area was the heart of the once wildly prosperous tin and copper mining area of West Cornwall. While you are in the area, consider taking the opportunity to go underground at Geevor Mine Museum and experience the sensation of the all enveloping darkness of a mine. Just along the coast from Geevor, and within walking distance, is Levant Mine where the National Trust and Trevithick Trust have preserved the last working mine steam engine in the county.

St Just

St Just was the capital of the mining district - it expanded rapidly after about 1840. Following the boom mining years of 1860's and 1870's it fell into an equally rapid decline. The place was pretty wild by all accounts with heavy drinking and obstreperous miners. It took John Wesley, with his fire and brimstone preaching, to subdue them. There was something in the hellfire which appealed to the Cornish spirit. The continuing importance of Methodism is symbolised by the grand view leading up to the Methodist chapel. In the centre of the village is a grassy amphitheatre - the Plen-an-Gwary. Medieval miracle plays were performed here and in recent years it has hosted the Cornish Ordinalia - a series of medieval plays based on the life of Christ and performed in Cornish.

Cape Cornwall

For many years until the Ordnance Survey proved otherwise, this was thought to be the most westerly point in the UK - hence it status as a 'cape' separating the English Channel and the Celtic Sea. Small boats work from Priest's Cove where there is also a small, sea filled, pool for children to paddle in. Every year, as part of Cape Games, a swimming race is held from the Brisons.

Portheras Cove

Pendeen Watch

The lighthouse guards the reefs of the Wra, pronounced 'ray' and is Cornish for 'witch'. Erected in 1900.

Kenidjack Castle

The ramparts on the north side of the headland guard Porthledden Cove which was a safe sandy landing beach in the Iron Age. The view to the west takes in the Isles of Scilly, Longships Lighthouse, Land's End and beyond to Cape Cornwall. To the north you can see the perilously positioned Crowns Engine Houses.

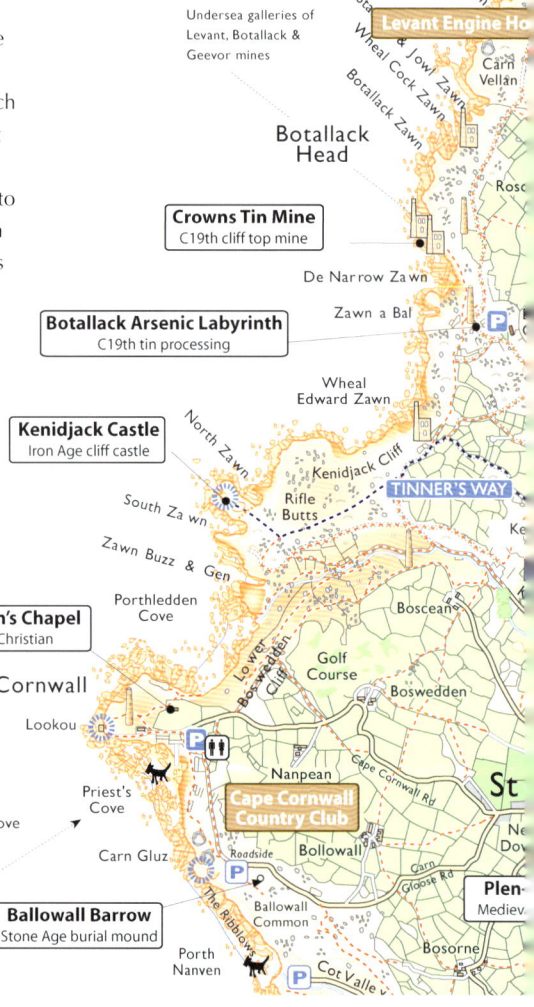

Undersea galleries of Levant, Botallack & Geevor mines

Levant Engine Ho

Carn
Vellan

Botallack
Head

Rosc

Crowns Tin Mine
C19th cliff top mine

De Narrow Zawn

Zawn a Bal

P

Botallack Arsenic Labyrinth
C19th tin processing

Wheal
Edward Zawn

Kenidjack Castle
Iron Age cliff castle

North Zawn

Kenidjack Cliff

TINNER'S WAY

Ke

South Zawn

Rifle
Butts

Zawn Buzz & Gen

Porthledden
Cove

Boscean

Golf
Course

Boswedden

St Helen's Chapel
Early Christian

Lower Boswedden Cliff

Cape Cornwall

Lookou

P

Nanpean

Cape Cornwall Rd

St

Ne
Dov

Priest's
Cove

Cape Cornwall
Country Club

Brisons to Priest's Cove
swimming race

Carn Gluz

Roadside

P

Bollowall

Carn
Gloose Rd

Plen
Mediev

Ballowall Barrow
Stone Age burial mound

Ballowall
Common

Bosorne

The Brisons

Porth
Nanven

The Ribbles

Cot Valley

P

The Wra
or
Three Stone Oar

The Mozens

Greeb Point

Blinker's
Bed

Zawn Alley

Manan

**Pendeen
Watch**

The
Kenidjacks

Pendeen Cove

Fox
Carn

Chair
Carn

Wolf Ro

Morvah
Cliff

Pendeen
New Cliff

Portheras
Cove

Carn Clough

Tregaminion Cliff

The Enys

Portheras Cliff

Chypraze

Lower Chypraze

Ens Zawn

Mill Zawn

Pendeen
House

Pendeen Old Cliff

Pendeen Vau
Iron Age Fogou

Higher Chypraze

Tregaminion

Morvah & Zennor

The Avarack

Manor
Farm

Chyrose
Farm

Rose Valley

Trewellard Zawn

Carn
Ros

White Gate
Cottage

Portheras
Farm

Calartha
Farm

Bojewyan

Keigwin

Ha
Dow

Trewellard
Bottoms

B3306

Portheras

Yew Tree
Gallery

Tor Noon

Lower
Boscaswell

Pendeen

Boje wyan
Stennack

P

Geevor Mine Museum

B3318

Chun Quoit
Stone Age (Neolithic) Tomb

Higher
Boscaswell

Boscaswell
Higher
Downs

Carn
Eanes

East
Bosca swell
Mine

Higher
Downs

Trewellard

Portheras
Common

B3318

Trewellard
Common

P

Woon Gumpus
Common

B3306

Portheras Common Barrow
Bronze Age burial mound

Carnyorth

Wheal Bal Hill

Carnyorth
Moor

Boslow Stone
Early Christian inscribed stone

Manor
Farm

Carn Bean

Botallack

Carnyorth
Common

Carn Kenidjack
or Hooting Carn

Truthwall

Truthwall
Common

Higher
Tregeseal

Kenython

Tregesal
Bronze Age stone circles

Valley

Tregeseal

TINNER'S WAY

Hailglower
Farm

lancherrow
Bridge

B3306

St Just
Rugby
Club

vary
heatre

A3071

Penzance & Land's End

Carn
Bosavern

rrallack

**Tregeseal Nine Maidens &
Kenidjack Carn**

Concentration of monuments including
stone circles, small holed stones and
Stone Age barrows. The carn is known
locally as Hooting Carn and is reputed to
be haunted.

Recommended Walks - The Tinner's Way

St Just

The Tinner's Way

West Cornwall has an unusually large number of well preserved ancient monuments and prehistoric villages. In ancient times these must have been linked by tracks and paths. Presumably they started off as tracks wandering across open land and they have since been fixed in the landscape by the building of granite hedges.

The majority of hedges we see today were built by the time of the Iron Age but some may have been ancient even then. One of the most complete tracks runs from Cape Cornwall towards St Ives, following the high ground above the north coast and linking many of the most impressive archaeological sites. This track is now popularly known as the Tinner's Way.

The whole walk can be done in a day by anyone who is fit but is more easily split into smaller sections each one becoming the basis for a number of other walks across the moors. The route can be walked in any direction starting either from St Ives or St Just. If you are walking the whole way from St Just it is more interesting to end the walk at Zennor because you can take in Zennor Hill and Quoit and finish at Zennor Head with its great views.

Most of the track is clear so detailed directions are not given here. You can usually get your bearings in relation to a few obvious landmarks es-pecially the old engine house on Greenbarrow Shaft of Ding Dong Mine. The coast road has a regular bus service in the summer between St Just and St Ives and you can get off almost anywhere and make your way up to the high ground and onto the track.

Tinner's Way - Part 1. Cape Cornwall & St Just to Kenidjack Carn

This walk is the start of the Tinner's Way to St Ives. It follows the high ground above the north coast and takes in many of the best ancient monuments in the Land's End peninsula.

Distance: 3 miles (2 hours).
Car parking: Cape Cornwall, Botallack, St Just & at the fork of the B3318 west of Chun Castle.
Buses: Regular buses from Penzance & St Ives to St Just.
Going: Easy.
Refreshments/Pubs: Pubs at Botallack, Pendeen & St Just.

Places to Visit

Geevor Mine Museum & Levant Mine

See 'Best Mining Sites to Visit' on page 42.

Things to Do

Lafrowda Festival

(P) & ⅋⅌⅓ ⅁⅂⅃ |⊙|

In July, a week long festival of street performers, giant paper and withy sculptures, banners and lanterns made in local schools.
www.lafrowda-festival.co.uk.

Cape Games

Annual race to the Brisons from Priest's Cove.

St Just Feast

(P) & ⅋⅌⅓ ⅁⅂⅃ |⊙|

November each year with Cornish wrestling.

Eating Out

Star Inn in St Just, meadery at Pendeen.

Treat Yourself....to a pint at the Star Inn in St Just.

If you do just one thing.... go down Geevor or Rosevale mines.

7. Morvah, Carn Galva & The Gurnard's Head

Carn Galva

This is the real, undiluted West Cornwall. The landscape is often bleak, but is never less than compelling in its grandeur. The colours in this landscape often seem heightened in comparison with the more sheltered south coast. In spring, fresh, delicate wild flowers make a perfect contrast with the solid, intimidating granite landscape and the massive stone walls of the local farms. In the autumn the hillsides turn a deep auburn as the bracken starts to die back.

Chun Castle

Unusually for West Cornwall, this Iron Age hillfort has stone ramparts rather than the more typical earth banks. The castle has been robbed of much of its stone but even in its present state it is quite imposing. The castle is constructed of three

concentric rings of ramparts originally standing up to 3 metres high.

The Gurnard's Head

The headland is only ten minutes walk from the Gurnard's Head pub at Treen. The Gurnard's Head can be an intimidating place to visit. It is not just the sheer cliff on the west side which always makes you wary - there is some sense of foreboding in the place. As with almost all headlands in Cornwall the Gurnard's Head was fortified with earth ramparts in the Iron Age. They are clearly visible on the narrow neck. You can stop in at the Gurnard's Head Hotel for a pint of Doom Bar Ale and Red Gurnard and chips.

At Lean Point you can see a small, water filled mine shaft cut into the rocks near sea level. The courtyard building here was associated with the pilchard industry.

Carn Galva & Ding Dong

It's a bit of a scrabble to get to the summit - especially in the summer when pushing through the gorse can make it a uncomfortably scratchy experience. Once you are through the gorse of the lower slopes and onto the granite outcrop itself the going becomes much easier. The view from outer carn is the best in the area. Carn Galva and the moorland that abruptly rise above the fields represent an ancient coastline at a time when sea levels were higher. The farmland on the shelf was then at beach level. Park at Carn Galva Mine or even better walk over the moors from Ding Dong Mine. Commando Ridge was used as a training area during the Second World War.

Bodrifty Prehistoric Village

Settlement of hut circles or round houses with a low defensive earthwork. Some of the hut circles may date from the late Bronze Age and it was certainly in occupation during the Iron Age. The site makes an interesting contrast with the more sophisticated later courtyard house settlements at Carn Euny and Chysauster. Invite yourself into one of the houses and take lunch in the exact spot and the way the original inhabitants would have done 2,000 years ago. More information on display boards around the site. There is a reconstructed round house near to Bodrifty Farm (picture p13) - follow the signs from Bodrifty Prehistoric Village.

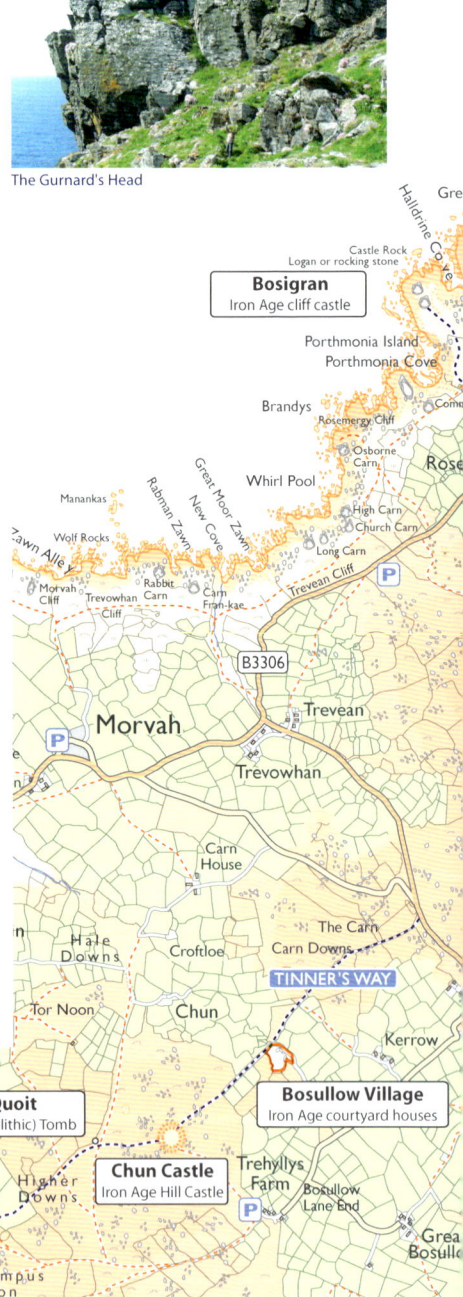

The Gurnard's Head

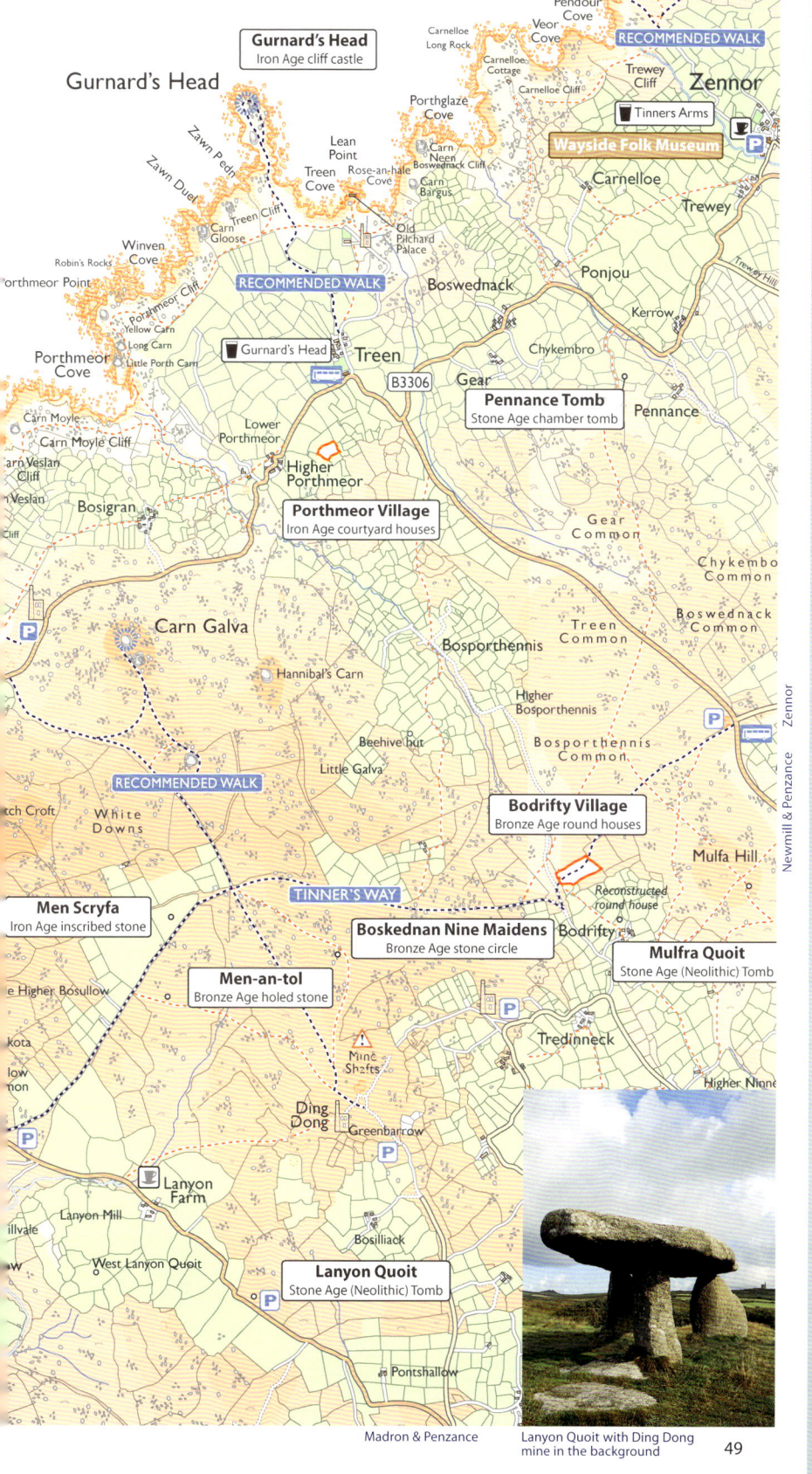

Gurnard's Head
Iron Age cliff castle

Gurnard's Head

RECOMMENDED WALK

Zennor

Tinners Arms

Wayside Folk Museum

Carnelloe

Trewey

Pendour Cove

Veor Cove

Carnelloe Long Rock

Carnelloe Cottage

Carnelloe Cliff

Porthglaze Cove

Carn Neen

Boswednack Cliff

Carn Bargus

Lean Point

Treen Cove

Rose-an-hale Cove

Zawn Pedn

Zawn Duel

Treen Cliff

Carn Gloose

Old Pilchard Palace

Boswednack

RECOMMENDED WALK

Winven Cove

Robin's Rocks

Porthmeor Point

Porthmeor Cliff

Yellow Carn

Long Carn

Little Porth Carn

Gurnard's Head Treen

B3306

Gear

Pennance Tomb
Stone Age chamber tomb

Pennance

Ponjou

Kerrow

Chykembro

Porthmeor Cove

Carn Moyle

Carn Moyle Cliff

Carn Veslan Cliff

Veslan Cliff

Bosigran

Lower Porthmeor

Higher Porthmeor

Porthmeor Village
Iron Age courtyard houses

Gear Common

Chykembo Common

Boswednack Common

Carn Galva

Hannibal's Carn

Bosporthennis

Higher Bosporthennis

Treen Common

Bosporthennis Common

Beehive hut

Little Galva

RECOMMENDED WALK

ch Croft

White Downs

Bodrifty Village
Bronze Age round houses

Mulfa Hill

Reconstructed round house

Men Scryfa
Iron Age inscribed stone

TINNER'S WAY

Boskednan Nine Maidens
Bronze Age stone circle

Bodrifty

Mulfra Quoit
Stone Age (Neolithic) Tomb

e Higher Bosullow

kota

low

non

Men-an-tol
Bronze Age holed stone

Tredinneck

Higher Ninne

Mine Shafts

Ding Dong

Greenbarrow

Lanyon Farm

Lanyon Mill

West Lanyon Quoit

illvale

w

Bosilliack

Lanyon Quoit
Stone Age (Neolithic) Tomb

Pontshallow

Madron & Penzance

Newmill & Penzance

Zennor

Lanyon Quoit with Ding Dong mine in the background

Recommended Walks around Carn Galva

Treen Cove with tin mine and pilchard palace

Ding Dong to Carn Galva

The mine building at Ding Dong competes with the ancient quoits to dominate the skyline on the moors. The walk takes you across the moors and then finishes with the magnificent view from Carn Galva over the coastal shelf. You can make diversions to both the Men-an-tol and Boskednan Nine Maidens stone circle.

Distance: 5km/3 miles round trip (2 hours).

Car parking: Roadside parking at Ding Dong (avoid the busy farm entrance) or park below Carn Galva.

Buses: Regular buses from St Ives to St Just on the coast road.

Going: Moderate - can be boggy after wet weather. Some climbing involved in getting onto Carn Galva.

Refreshments/Pubs: Nothing on route. Nearest pubs - The Gurnard's Head (Cornish fish soup particularly recommended) and the Tinner's Arms at Zennor.

Tinner's Way - Part 2. Chun to Mulfra Quoit

This easy section is neatly topped and tailed by two Stone Age tombs with an archaeology lesson in between. Almost all of the really famous monuments are on this section **Distance:** 7km/4.5 miles (3 hours). **Car parking:** Car park at the fork of the B3318 west of Chun Castle, at Trehyllys Farm below Chun Castle and opposite Men-an-tol Studio. **Buses:** Regular buses from St Ives to St Just on the coast road and occasional bus service from Newmill to Penzance. **Going:** Moderate - can be tough going when the bracken is fully grown. **Refreshments/Pubs:** Nothing on route - Gurnard's Head and Tinner's Arms.

The entrance to Chun Castle

Places to Visit
Wayside Museum, Zennor
Small and intimate award winning museum, illustrating the life of local working people in the last century.

Things to Do
Picnics & walks
Almost every walk in this section ends with a view or a monument.

Eating Out
The Gurnard's Head and Tinner's arms at Zennor.
If you do just one thing....
take in the view from the top of Carn Galva.

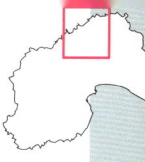

St Senara's Church in Zennor village

This final part of the coastline before St Ives is centred around the hamlet of Zennor. The village is a perfect starting and finishing point for all explorations in this section. Whether that is a gentle stroll down to Zennor Head in the evening to watch the sun set, or a longer walk across the high ground to Zennor Quoit, all to be finished in the Tinner's Arms. This section has two ancient villages - the Bronze Age round houses of Bodrifty and the plush Iron Age courtyard houses of Chysauster.

Zennor

St Senara, after which the village is named, was a beautiful and virtuous Breton princess married to a prince of Brittany. Her jealous stepmother wrongly accused her of infidelity and she was condemned death by drowning. She was only saved when she said she was pregnant. Fearing they would be accused of killing an innocent baby, as well as Senara, they threw the princess in to the sea in a barrel. She was swept to Ireland - giving birth to a son on the way and being fed by the gulls and sea creatures. Senara and her son, Budoc, returned to Brittany many years later when the stepmother was exposed as a witch. On their way to Brittany they stopped here and founded the parishes of Zennor and Budock near Falmouth. Rising above Zennor is Churchtown Common and Zennor Hill with wide views along the coast. It's best to visit in the evening, perhaps taking a picnic to the top. A number of paths lead up to Zennor Hill & Sperris Croft. The quickest way up is by the path that leaves the main road just up from the red telephone box. This is quite a scramble. Alternatively you can walk up the track opposite Eagle's Nest - the former home of the artist Patrick Heron.

The track to Zennor Hill and Quoit looking over Eagles Nest

Little Carracks

The Carracks

Treveal Cove

Economy Cove

Treveal Cliff

Mussel Point

Cornelias Zawn

Wicca Pool

Trilley Rock

Carn Porth

Wicca Cliff

RE

Gala Rocks

Wicca

Zennor Head

Tregerthan Cliff

Porthzennor Cove

Tremeader Cliff

Tregerthen

Horseback Zawn

Zennor Cliff

Tremeader

RECOMMENDED WALK

Higher Tregerthen

Pendour Cove

Veor Cove

Church Path

Carnelloe Long Rock

Trewey Cliff

Zennor

Eagles Nest

Carnelloe Cottage

Carnelloe Cliff

🍺 Tinners Arms

B3306

Tremeader Common

Porthglaze Cove

🏛 **Wayside Folk Museum**

🅿

Zennor Hill

Churchtown Common

Carn Neen

Boswednack Cliff

Carnelloe

Rosevale

The Carne

an-hale ove

Carn Bargus

Trewey

Rosevale Mine

Rosemorran

Old Pitchard Palace

Ponjou

Zennor Quoit
Stone Age (Neolithic) Tomb

Boswednack

Kerrow

Foage

Chykembro

Trewey Hill

B3306

Gear

Pennance

Pennance Tomb
Stone Age chamber tomb

⚠ Mine Shafts

Trewey Common

Mill Downs

Gear Common

Chykembro Common

⚠ Mine Shafts

TINNER'S WAY

Boswednack Common

Treen Common

Kerrowe

Bosporthennis

Higher Kerrowe

Bishop's Head & Foot

Tum

Higher Bosporthennis

🅿 🚌

Higher Trye

Coast road to Morvah, Pendeen & St Just

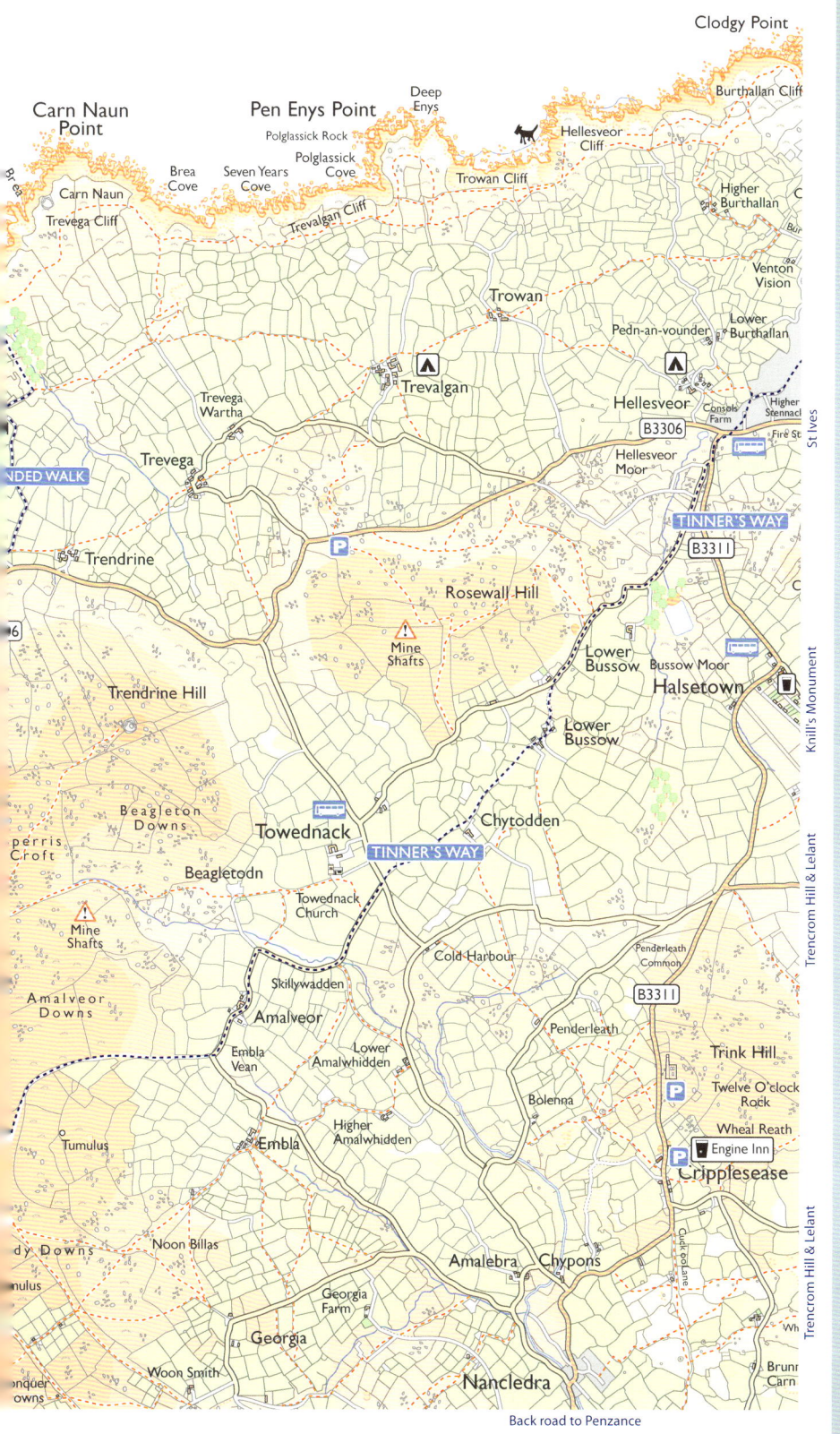

Clodgy Point

Burthallan Cliff

Carn Naun Point

Pen Enys Point

Deep Enys

Polglassick Rock

Hellesveor Cliff

Brea Cove

Seven Years Cove

Polglassick Cove

Trevalgan Cliff

Trowan Cliff

Higher Burthallan

Carn Naun

Trevega Cliff

Venton Vision

Trowan

Pedn-an-vounder

Lower Burthallan

Trevega Wartha

Trevalgan

Hellesveor

Consols Farm

Higher Stennack

St Ives

Trevega

B3306

Hellesveor Moor

Fire St

ROUNDED WALK

Trendrine

Rosewall Hill

P

TINNER'S WAY

B3311

6

Trendrine Hill

Mine Shafts

Lower Bussow

Bussow Moor

Halsetown

Knill's Monument

Lower Bussow

Beagleton Downs

Chytodden

Towednack

TINNER'S WAY

perris Croft

Beagletodn

Towednack Church

Cold Harbour

Penderleath Common

Trencrom Hill & Lelant

Mine Shafts

Skillywadden

Penderleath

B3311

Amalveor Downs

Amalveor

Trink Hill

Embla Vean

Lower Amalwhidden

Bolenna

Twelve O'clock Rock

Tumulus

Higher Amalwhidden

Wheal Reath

Embla

Engine Inn

Cripplesease

dy Downs

Noon Billas

Clodgy Lane

Amalebra

Chypons

mulus

Georgia Farm

Georgia

Brunn Carn

Woon Smith

onquer owns

Nancledra

Wh

8. Mulfra & Zennor to St Ives

The Mermaid of Zennor

Morvennor, a mermaid princess and daughter of the sea, fell in love with a Zennor lad called Matthew Trewella after hearing his singing carried by the wind down to the sea from the church. She disguised herself and enticed him into the sea at Pendour Cove. His family tired to stop him, but he walked after Morvennor - entranced by her beauty. His mother was the last person to see him. On a still night, if you listen carefully, you can hear him serenading his wife. You might also catch sight of his mother patiently waiting for him to return.

Recommended Walks around Zennor

Tinner's Way - Part 3. Mulfra to Towednack

Zennor Quoit

This last part of the Tinner's Way crosses the moors behind the impressive hills of Zennor, Trendrine and Rosewall before descending to the fields around Towednack and then finishing on the outskirts of St Ives. You can make diversions off the main route to both Chysauster Ancient Village and Zennor Quoit. The hills themselves are worth visiting for the views and all are topped by ruined tombs of the Ancients. **Distance:** 4km/2.5 miles (Mulfra to Towednack) 2 hours. **Car parking:** Limited verge side parking opposite the turning towards Higher Kerrowe Farm and on the north side of Rosewall hill. **Buses:** Regular buses from St Ives to St Just on the coast road plus St Ives/Pz bus via Newmill. **Going:** Moderate - can be tough going when the bracken is fully grown. **Refreshments/Pubs:** Tinner's Arms and Chapel Cafe at Zennor, the Halsetown Inn.

Wicca Pool & River Cove

This walk follows one of the few shelter, wooded valleys on the north coast. Seals are often seen basking on the Carracks. **Distance**: 5km/3 miles round trip - 2 hours. **Going**: The path from Wicca Farm to River Cove is fairly easy. Once on the coast path things become more strenuous as the path falls to Economy Cove and then rises sharply above Wicca Pool. **Car parking**: small car park at Wicca Farm: **Refreshments**: tea, cakes and beer at Zennor. From the car park at Wicca, return along the lane towards Boscubben. Turn down the tarmac road to Treveal and the follow the National Trust signs to Trevail Mill and River Cove.

Places to Visit
Wayside Museum, Zennor
Small and intimate award winning museum, illustrating the life of local working people in the last century.

Things to Do
Take a pasty and watch seals at Treveal Cove of explore the hills behind Zennor.

Eating Out
The Gurnard's Head and the Chapel Cafe and the Tinner's arms at Zennor.

Treat Yourself.... to an evening picnic at Zennor Head followed by a night in the Tinner's Arms at Zennor.

If you do just one thing.... meet the ancients at Chysauster Ancient Village.

9. St Ives & Trencrom

St Ia's Chapel on the The Island at St Ives

In this final section we leave the remote north coast and its scattered farm settlements and enter the shelter of St Ives Bay. The bay comes into view as a great crescent of sandy beaches that stretch round from St Ives to Godrevy Lighthouse. During the 1940's St Ives became an international centre for modern abstract painters and sculptors. They later became known as the St Ives School. The opening of the Tate Gallery in 1993 celebrates their work.

Trencrom Hill

Trencrom Hill was the legendary home of Giant Trencobn brother of Giant Cormoron who lived on St Michael's Mount. They used to pass the time of day by throwing stones to one another and are supposed to have built the walls of Trencrom Castle. The hill is supposed to be hollow and inhabited by spriggins - a mischievous race of pixies who stole the tools of tin miners unless they were left the crimp of their pasties. Modern archaeology takes a different view and tells us that Trencrom is probably a Neolithic settlement with later, Iron Age, defensive banks on the south and west. It is sited to dominate the Hayle estuary - an important trade route in prehistoric times and there are certainly great views across St Ives Bay to Godrevy Lighthouse.

It's a great place to take a picnic and children love to play in the grassy depressions on the summit - actually the remains of ancient round houses. After you have been to the top, walk down to Higher Hill Woods where there are lots of trees for children to climb.

In the spring the hill is fragrant with the coconut smell of Gorse flowers and in the autumn it's a favourite place to pick blackberries.

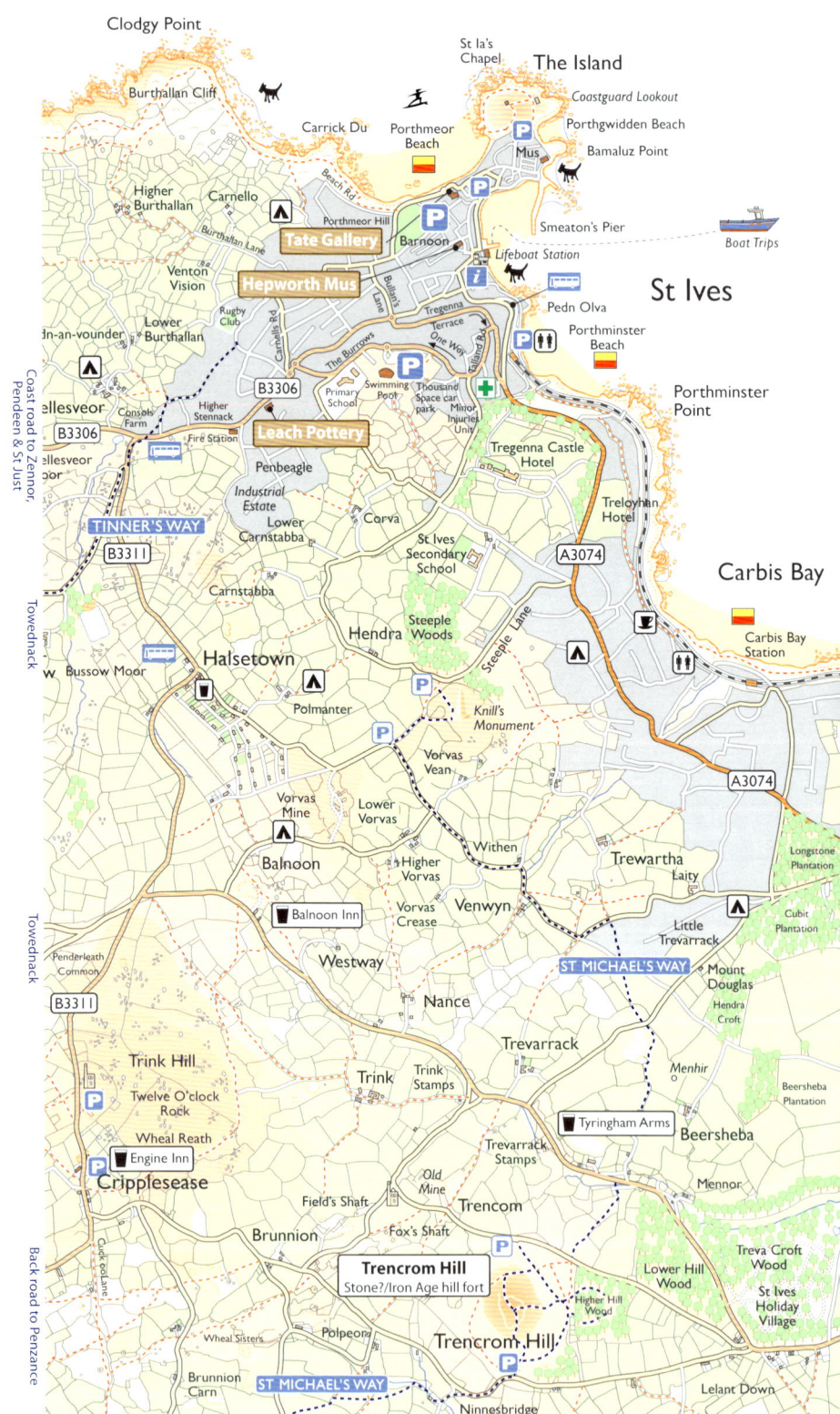

Clodgy Point

Burthallan Cliff

Carrick Du

St Ia's Chapel

The Island

Porthmeor Beach

Coastguard Lookout

Porthgwidden Beach

Bamaluz Point

Mus

Higher Burthallan

Carnello

Higher Stennack

Porthmeor Hill

Beach Rd

Burthallan Lane

Tate Gallery

Barnoon

Smeaton's Pier

Boat Trips

Venton Vision

Hepworth Mus

Lifeboat Station

St Ives

Rugby Club

Pedn Olva

Porthminster Beach

Lower Burthallan

dn-an-vounder

Tregenna Terrace

One Way

Porthminster Point

Coast road to Zennor, Pendeen & St Just

llesveor

Consols Farm

The Burrows

B3306

Primary School

Swimming Pool

Thousand Space car park

Minor Injuries Unit

Leach Pottery

Fire Station

Tregenna Castle Hotel

B3306

llesveor oor

Penbeagle

Industrial Estate

Corva

St Ives Secondary School

Treloyhan Hotel

TINNER'S WAY

Lower Carnstabba

A3074

Carbis Bay

B3311

Carnstabba

Hendra

Steeple Woods

Carbis Bay Station

Bussow Moor

Halsetown

Polmanter

Knill's Monument

Steeple Lane

A3074

Vorvas Vean

Longstone Plantation

Vorvas Mine

Lower Vorvas

Withen

Trewartha

Laity

Cubit Plantation

Balnoon

Higher Vorvas

Venwyn

Vorvas Crease

Balnoon Inn

Little Trevarrack

Mount Douglas

Westway

Nance

ST MICHAEL'S WAY

Hendra Croft

B3311

Penderleath Common

Trevarrack

Menhir

Beersheba Plantation

Trink Hill

Trink

Trink Stamps

Beersheba

Twelve O'clock Rock

Wheal Reath

Tyringham Arms

Trevarrack Stamps

Engine Inn

Mennor

Cripplesease

Field's Shaft

Old Mine

Trencom

Treva Croft Wood

Brunnion

Fox's Shaft

Lower Hill Wood

St Ives Holiday Village

Trencrom Hill
Stone?/Iron Age hill fort

Higher Hill Wood

Wheal Sisters

Polpeor

Trencrom Hill

Brunnion Carn

ST MICHAEL'S WAY

Ninnesbridge

Lelant Down

Back road to Penzance

Towednack

Towednack

St Ives

St Ives was founded by St Ia, a Celtic saint who sailed from Ireland to St Ives on a leaf in C6th. Her chapel stands on the Island looking out to sea and her church watches over the spacious harbour. She is especially revered as a protector of fishermen. St Ives prospered on the twin industries of fishing and mining in the C19th. Many of the attractive courtyards in the town are former pilchard palaces where fish were gutted, pressed and salted (see Newlyn Pilchards in Section 1). Small fishing boats still work out of the harbour on the local reefs and there are good fish restaurants in the town.

The town benefits from an extraordinary bright and piercing light which is said to be the result of sunlight reflecting off the surrounding sea. It was partly this quality of light, and the picturesque appearance of the town, that first attracted artists to St Ives.

During July and August the small streets are packed with visitors - it's impossible even to push a child's buggy through the town. Don't be afraid to avoid the main streets and get yourself lost in the lovely little back streets. If you are visiting in the summer, consider arriving early in the morning or late in the evening when the crowds have dispersed. In fact, St Ives is at its glorious best in the late autumn and winter when the bracken on the surrounding moors is at its deepest auburn and the skies are at their most dramatic.

It's best to avoid driving into St Ives in the summer as the few car parks fill up very quickly. If you have to drive, aim for the 1000 space car park next to the swimming pool. A better option is to take the train from Penzance, St Erth, or from the park and ride at Lelant Saltings - you get great views over St Ives Bay.

St Ives harbour

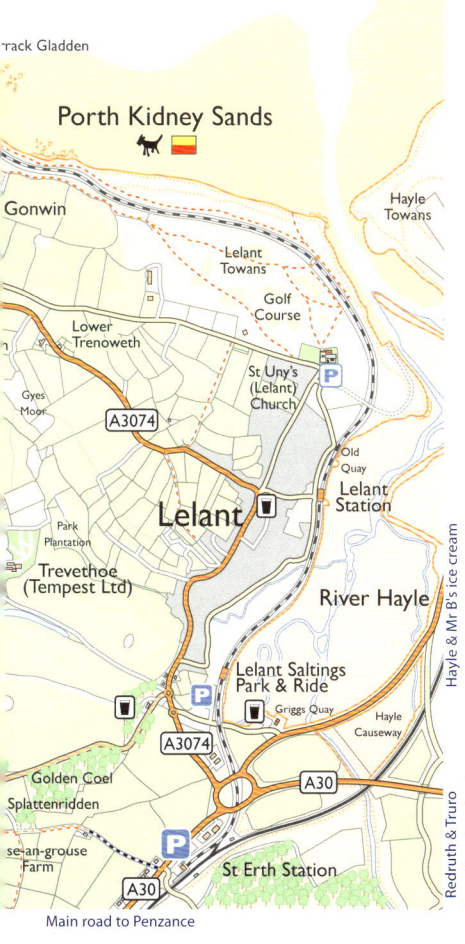

The St Ives School - Painters, Potters & Sculptors

When the railway reached Cornwall in the late C19th it brought with it the first of many writers and artists attracted to the remote villages of West Cornwall. This Victorian movement was mainly based around the fishing ports of Newlyn and Lamorna on the south coast (see Pilchards & Painters in Section 1). The themes for their paintings came directly from the lives of the working fishing communities. Their work is permanently on show at Penlee House Museum and Gallery in Penzance.

The St Ives School was a different sort of undertaking. In the decade before the Second World War a group of artists, included Roger Hilton, Ben Nicholson, Christopher Wood and the sculptor Barbara Hepworth gathered in St Ives. These artists shared a common interest in pushing their work towards abstraction based on European modernism. They found inspiration in the granite landscape with its bold shapes and strong colours.

A vital spur to these artists was the discovery of the paintings of a retired St Ives fisherman called Alfred Wallis.

Wallis had no formal artistic education and did not start painting until late in his life. Ben Nicholson and Christopher Wood came across his work quite by accident when visiting St Ives in 1928. They caught sight of him painting, through the open door of his house near Porthmeor beach, while out walking one day. The naive painting style of Alfred Wallis was an inspiration to them and it helped to confirm Wood and Nicholson in a more abstract approach to their own work. Something they later developed in Paris while working with Mondrian and Picasso.

Nicholson and Hepworth settled in St Ives during the Second World War and the group were joined for a short period by the hugely influential Jewish artist Naum Gabo - a refugee from Nazi Germany. Gabo became a catalyst for a what became briefly in the 1940's and 1950's an internationally recognised centre for abstract art. The group also included the painters Peter Lanyon, Terry Frost and Patrick Heron who worked here for the rest of their lives. It was to show the work of these artists that the Tate opened the St Ives Tate in 1993.

Terry Frost - Green, Black and White Movement 1951

Tate St Ives © Estate of Terry Frost

St Ives - Places to Visit, Things To Do

Tate St Ives

Ⓟ (Balnoon) ♿ 🚻 ♿ 🍴

An extraordinary success since it opened in 1993 - attracting many thousands of visitors. Shows the work of the St Ives School and has changing exhibitions of contemporary artists, guided talks of the gallery, family activities, cafe and shop. £1 off admission for rail park & ride ticket holders.
T: (01736) 796226
www.tate.org.uk/stives

Hepworth Museum & Sculpture Garden

Also part of the Tate, this was the studio garden and home of Barbara Hepworth. Her works call to mind the monumental Bronze Age standing stones of West Cornwall.
T: (01736) 796226
www.tate.org.uk/stives/hepworth

St Ives Museum

I love this museum - lots of objects from the history of St Ives. A captivating history of the Hain Steamship Company which operated from the town for over 100 years. Started in the days of sail, it trained many local boys to become seamen and captains. The company reached its peak before the First World War - controlling a fleet of forty ocean-going steamships. Nearly half were lost in the war.
T: (01736) 796005

Leach Pottery

Recently refurbished and expanded, this is the studio of the potter Bernard Leach - whose work can also be seen in the Tate St Ives. Born in the Far East, came to St Ives in 1920 with Shoji Hamada and set up this studio pottery using the techniques he had learnt in Japan. Shuttle bus runs between the Tate and the pottery during the summer.
T: (01736) 799703
www.leachpottery.com

ALFRED WALLIS
ARTIST & MARINER
1855–1942
LIVED HERE

Art Galleries

St Ives has a huge number of galleries - try the New Millennium Gallery in Street-an-Pol (opposite the Tourist Information Centre) for contemporary artists (www.newmillennium-gallery.co.uk) and the New Craftsman Gallery.

Things to Do

St Ives Swimming Pool

Follow signs to the 1,000 space car park. T: (01736) 797006

September Festival

Lots and lots of music. www.stivesseptemberfestival.co.uk or call St Ives TIC.

Boat Trips

To watch seals - look for the boards near the lifeboat station. Boat hire from here also.

Surf Schools

On Porthmeor beach.

Art Pass

The Art Pass gives seven days unlimited access to six West Cornwall galleries - Tate St Ives, Barbara Hepworth Museum and Sculpture Garden, Leach Pottery, Penlee House Gallery & Museum, and Newlyn Art Gallery & the Exchange.

Eating Out

St Ives has a long list of good places to eat.

Treat Yourself...

...to lunch at the Porthminster Cafe and a picture from one of the art galleries in St Ives.

If you do just one thing....

...the Barbara Hepworth Museum does it for me.

Porthgwidden beach

Natural History in West Cornwall

Coast Plants & Habitats

The presence of the surrounding sea has a moderating effect in the sheltered valleys and gardens of West Cornwall that allows tender plants to thrive here. But there is also a less benign effect of being on the coast. The salty westerly gales that blow uninterrupted from the Azores, desiccate and burn any exposed soft leaves in their path. As a result few trees are able to survive outside the sheltered valleys. Those that do, have their buds pruned on the exposed side leaving the trees lopsided so that even on a still day they look as if they are being blown by a gale.

This is an overwhelmingly hostile environment for most common inland plants, but is an opportunity for others that have evolved to thrive on the exposed cliffs. These coastal specialists are part of the great appeal of the cliffs. Loss of moisture is the main problem for any plant in this habitat and a whole ecosystem of specialised plants and animals have adapted to overcome this problem. In fact, many coastal plants are so completely adapted they are unable to grow or compete in more sheltered areas. Some species like the fern Sea Spleenwort have never been found more that a few hundred metres from the sea.

Most maritime plants are adapted to retain precious moisture and in this respect mimic the adaptations of desert plants. The beautiful, blousy, Sea Campion illustrates this adaptation when com-pared with its inland cousin, Bladder Campion. Sea Campion has waxy, fleshy leaves that reduce transpiration and help to store water.

Sea Campion

Many plants like Heather adopt a low growing or prostrate habit on the cliffs. As they are nearer to the ground, wind speed is slower, and the resulting increased ground cover reduces drying out of the soil. In the most exposed areas dwarf varieties predominate - this helps the plant by reducing the area of tissue exposed to the drying wind. There are tiny Sea Carrot plants on the exposed side of Logan Rock. Another common strategy is to have short growing season triggered by favourable growing conditions and most coastal plants are in flower by May before the summer really takes hold.

Sea Carrot

In a difficult habitat where nutrients are in short supply on the poor soils, some plants gain advantage by taking food from other species. Coastal habitats have a fascinating collection of parasitic plants. On Gwennap Head in spring you can see the small pink flowers of Lousewort which supplements its own food production by sucking the sap from the roots of Heather. At Land's End, Gwennap Head and Logan Rock the Gorse is often matted by the pink threads of the parasitic Dodder plant. It is totally dependent on gorse sap for all its nutrients.

Lousewort a parasite on Heather

The real unsung heroes of the coast are the lichens which thrive in the clean moist air creating the wonderful bearded

The pink flowers of Dodder